ROUTLEDGE LIBRARY EDITIONS: LIBRARY AND INFORMATION SCIENCE

Volume 80

ROLE OF SERIALS IN SCI-TECH LIBRARIES

ROLE OF SERIALS IN SCI-TECH LIBRARIES

Edited by
ELLIS MOUNT

LONDON AND NEW YORK

First published in 1983 by The Haworth Press, Inc.

This edition first published in 2020
by Routledge
2 Park Square, Milton Park, Abingdon, Oxon OX14 4RN

and by Routledge
52 Vanderbilt Avenue, New York, NY 10017

Routledge is an imprint of the Taylor & Francis Group, an informa business

© 1983 The Haworth Press, Inc.

All rights reserved. No part of this book may be reprinted or reproduced or utilised in any form or by any electronic, mechanical, or other means, now known or hereafter invented, including photocopying and recording, or in any information storage or retrieval system, without permission in writing from the publishers.

Trademark notice: Product or corporate names may be trademarks or registered trademarks, and are used only for identification and explanation without intent to infringe.

British Library Cataloguing in Publication Data
A catalogue record for this book is available from the British Library

ISBN: 978-0-367-34616-4 (Set)
ISBN: 978-0-429-34352-0 (Set) (ebk)
ISBN: 978-0-367-36329-1 (Volume 80) (hbk)
ISBN: 978-0-367-36331-4 (Volume 80) (pbk)
ISBN: 978-0-429-34534-0 (Volume 80) (ebk)

Publisher's Note
The publisher has gone to great lengths to ensure the quality of this reprint but points out that some imperfections in the original copies may be apparent.

Disclaimer
The publisher has made every effort to trace copyright holders and would welcome correspondence from those they have been unable to trace.

Role of Serials in Sci-Tech Libraries

Ellis Mount, Editor

The Haworth Press
New York

Role of Serials in Sci-Tech Libraries has also been published as *Science & Technology Libraries*, volume 4, number 1, Fall 1983.

Copyright © 1983 by The Haworth Press, Inc. All rights reserved. Copies of articles in this publication may be reproduced noncommercially for the purpose of educational or scientific advancement. Otherwise, no part of this work may be reproduced or utilized in any form or by any means, electronic or mechanical including photocopying, microfilm, and recording, or by any information storage and retrieval system, without permission in writing from the publisher. Printed in the United States of America.

The Haworth Press, Inc., 28 East 22 Street, New York, NY 10010

Library of Congress Cataloging in Publication Data
Main entry under title:

Role of serials in sci-tech libraries.

"Has also been published as Science & technology libraries, volume 4, number 1, fall 1983"—T.p. verso.
Includes bibliographical references.
1. Scientific libraries—Addresses, essays, lectures. 2. Technical libraries—Addresses, essays, lectures. 3. Serials control systems—Addresses, essays, lectures. 4. Science—Periodicals—Evaluation—Addresses, essays, lectures. 5. Technology—Periodicals—Evaluation—Addresses, essays, lectures. I. Mount, Ellis.
Z675.T3R559 1983   026'.6   83-12682
ISBN 0-86656-260-5

Role of Serials in Sci-Tech Libraries

Science & Technology Libraries
Volume 4, Number 1

CONTENTS

Introduction *Ellis Mount, Editor*	1
Scientific and Technical Journals: Developments and Prospects *K. Subramanyam*	3
A Computer-Based Routing System for Serials *Rita L. Goodemote*	21
Choosing and Using Subscription Agents in Sci-Tech Libraries: Theory and Practice *Sheila S. Intner*	31
Selection and Evaluation of Chemistry Periodicals *Barbara A. Rice*	43
Selecting Multispecialty Mathematics Research Journals via Their Underlying Subject Emphases *Tony Stankus* *Virgil Diodato*	61
Pharmacy Faculty Members' Exposure to Current Periodicals *Wendell A. Guy*	79
Publishing—A View on Science/Technology Information (STI) Transfer *David L. Staiger*	85

SPECIAL PAPER

The In-House Translator: An Overlooked Specialist   91
    Patricia E. Newman

SCI-TECH ONLINE   99
    Ellen Nagle, Editor

SCI-TECH IN REVIEW   105
    Suzanne Fedunok, Editor

Introduction

It is apparent to all those even slightly acquainted with sci-tech libraries and information centers that serials, including journals, are of prime importance to such organizations. Despite their costs and the problems involved in selecting, handling and storing such literature, serials remain the key source of information for most scientists and engineers. Thus, it is only fitting that an issue of this journal be devoted to sci-tech serials.

An overall view of the history, development and outlook for sci-tech journals is given in K. Subramanyam's paper. The development of a computer-based system for routing serials in a network of corporate libraries is described in Rita L. Goodemote's paper. Choosing a subscription agent is included in Sheila S. Intner's discussion and research study of the pros and cons of obtaining serial subscriptions with or without agents.

Three papers deal with the selection and/or evaluation of sci-tech serials, the first concerning chemistry periodicals, is discussed by Barbara A. Rice. Selection of mathematics journals is the topic of a paper co-authored by Tony Stankus and Virgil Diodato. Selection of pharmacy journals is the theme of the contribution by Wendell A. Guy.

The Special Paper for this issue consists of a description, by Patricia E. Newman, of the nature of the duties and the qualifications of in-house translators, a welcome supplement to our issue (v. 3 no. 2) on the *Role of Translations in Sci-Tech Libraries*.

The last paper, by David L. Staiger, discusses the changing nature of sci-tech printing and publishing, including the role played by serials, as technologies bring new situations.

The issue includes our standard features, with the exception of "New Reference Works" which will resume with a new Editor in our next issue.

Ellis Mount

Scientific and Technical Journals: Developments and Prospects

K. Subramanyam

I. INTRODUCTION

The *Librarians' Glossary* defines a periodical as:

A publication with a distinctive title which appears at stated or regular intervals, generally oftener than once a year, without prior decision as to when the last issue shall appear. It contains articles, stories or other writings, by several contributors. Newspapers, whose chief function is to disseminate news, and the memoirs, proceedings, journals, etc. of societies are not considered periodicals under the cataloguing rules. . . . At the General Conference of Unesco, held at Paris on 19th November 1964, it was agreed that a publication is a periodical if it constitutes one issue in a continuous series under the same title, published at regular or irregular intervals, over an indefinite period, individual issues in the series being numbered consecutively or each issue being dated.[1]

Various cataloging codes, such as the *Anglo-American Cataloguing Rules,* give differing definitions of serials and periodicals. Most definitions agree that serials include periodicals, as well as such other types of continuing publications as annuals, yearbooks, almanacs, proceedings, government publications, newspapers, newsletters, continuations, directories, etc.

A further distinction is made between journals and magazines; both are periodicals, but "magazines are written chiefly for the general reader, whereas journals are for readers specialized in a

---

K. Subramanyam is associate professor, School of Library and Information Science, Drexel University, Philadelphia, PA 19104. He received his MLS and PhD degrees in library and information science from the University of Pittsburgh.

particular discipline or interested in intellectually sophisticated treatments of a variety of subjects."[2] There is considerable diversity and confusion in the definitions of serials and periodicals. Machlup, Leeson and associates have examined several definitions, and suggested a categorization of serials.[3]

The rest of this paper is mainly concerned with the primary scientific journal, containing largely, but not exclusively, research papers.

II. HISTORICAL OVERVIEW

Private correspondence was the predominant means of scientific communication until the middle of the 17th century. As a medium for exchanging scientific information, personal correspondence had many defects:

1. Much time and effort were needed to write letters.
2. Letters were personal in tone, and were not sent to those who would disagree with or debate their contents.
3. Unsound theories were not objectively criticized and rejected.
4. Questions of priority could not be resolved satisfactorily.
5. Some writers invented ciphers or systems of shorthand to maintain secrecy.
6. Many people who were interested in science did not receive letters.

Though the idea of a scientific journal was mooted by Sir Robert Moray, President of the Royal Society, in 1661, it was in France that the first journal started. The first weekly issue of the *Journal des Scavans* was published on January 5, 1665. One of the objectives of the *Journal* was "to make known experiments in physics, chemistry, and anatomy that may serve to explain natural phenomena, to describe useful or curious inventions of machines, and to record meteorological data."[4]

When the *Journal des Scavans* was being established in France, plans were under way in England to publish a scientific periodical to report the accounts of scientific experiments, excluding legal and theological matters. Under the aegis of the Royal Society, the first issue of the *Philosophical Transactions* appeared on Monday, March 6, 1665. In spite of several handicaps in its early years, the

Philosophical Transactions has survived for over three centuries and has published some of the most illustrious scientific papers including those of Herschel, Priestley, Franklin, Rumford, and Henry Cavendish.

The *Journal des Scavans* and the *Philosophical Transactions* served as models for subsequent scientific periodicals of European societies and academies. One of the first journals that followed this model was the Latin journal *Acta Eruditorum* (1682-) published at Leipzig. Many papers of Leitnitz on calculus were published in this journal. The number of scientific and technical journals increased slowly at first, and more and more rapidly during the 19th and 20th centuries. By 1800, there were about 90 scientific periodicals worldwide. The early history of scientific and technical periodicals has been studied by Kronick, McKie, and others.[5,6]

For over three centuries, the scientific journal, in its format now familiar to us, has remained one of the most important channels for the communication of scientific and technical information. However, from time to time, suggestions have been made to alter its traditional format or to replace the journal with alternative mechanisms for the dissemination of scientific information. The following are some of the proposals suggesting drastic augmentations or alternatives to the primary journal put forward in the last three decades:

1. Organization of information exchange groups for public distribution or preprints.[7,8]
2. On-demand distribution of author-prepared summaries and/or full papers.[9]
3. Repackaging of primary journals into ''user journals'' or ''super journals'' for particular user groups.[10]
4. Establishment of separate radio stations and/or television stations for broadcasting science reports.
5. Distribution of research reports on tape recordings.
6. Substitution of the primary journal by the individual paper (or ''separate'') as the primary unit of distribution.

Extensively documented reports of these and similar other proposals have been made by Phelps and Hills.[11,12] By far the most momentous alternative to the scientific journal yet suggested is the substitution of the individual paper or ''separate'' as the primary unit of distribution. Variations of this proposal, and their merits and disadvantages have been discussed elsewhere.[13] Despite several alternatives proposed from time to time, the scientific journal has continued to gain acceptance as the most important formal channel for the dissemination of scientific and technical information.

III. IMPORTANCE OF JOURNALS IN SCIENTIFIC AND TECHNICAL COMMUNICATION

The scientific journal serves three important functions.[14] First of all, it serves as an archival record of scientific scholarship, scrutinized and validated by scientists. Refereed papers published in journals constitute the basic source material for consolidation and compaction into textbooks, reviews, handbooks, encyclopedias, and similar other secondary packages.

Secondly, the journal is a medium for disseminating current information. Besides the results of research and development activity, the journal conveys a variety of information—historical, social, political, commercial, and pedagogical information—of interest to scientists. Scientists depend on the journal as a medium through which they can keep themselves abreast of current developments in scientific research.

Lastly, the primary journal is a social institution that confers prestige and rewards on authors, editors, referees, subscribers, and publishers. Published papers are considered as a tangible measure of scientists' contribution to the advancement of scientific knowledge, and as a basis for an evaluation of their work by their peers and employers. Publication of the results of research and development in journals facilitates the establishment of priority and ownership of ideas and discoveries. The journal also confers recognition and prestige on editors and referees.

IV. PROBLEMS OF THE SCIENTIFIC JOURNAL

Despite its important place in science communication, the primary journal has been the subject of severe criticism on account of its many drawbacks. The efficiency of the journal as a channel for communicating scientific information has suffered because of its uncontrolled growth resulting in overfragmentation and scattering of primary scientific literature. Due to the diversity of its additional functions, some of which are often mutually conflicting, the journal has become too general and expensive a package, unable to perform any of its functions efficiently. The delay in its production necessitated by its role as a validated archival record of science, is severely restricting its function as a current awareness tool. The following are some of the problems that have invited repeated criticism.

A. Proliferation

Concern over the uncontrolled proliferation of journals is not new. "In 1716, apprehension was felt about the overpopulation of periodicals whose remainder would have to be bundled up and sold like rotten cheese."[15] Estimates of the number of scientific and technical periodicals in existence vary from 26,000 to 100,000 titles.[16-18] The fourth edition of the *World List of Scientific Periodicals* (London: Butterworths, 1963-1975) lists 59,961 titles. K. P. Barr argues that "the number of currently available scientific and technical periodicals which contain material of interest to the practising scientists and technologists is 26,000."[19] King and others have estimated that the number of scientific and technical periodicals worldwide would be close to 70,000 by 1985.[20]

The proliferation of scientific journals may be ascribed to various factors:

1. Increase in research and development activity worldwide.
2. Increase in the number of scientists active in research and development and in publishing.
3. Importance attached to publications as a measure of a scientist's contribution.
4. Increasing specialization and compartmentalization of science.
5. Developments in the technology of printing and publishing.

Proliferation of journal literature is due not only to the birth of new journals, but also to the "splitting" of a journal into several sections that eventually become separate journals. For example, the *Transactions of the American Society of Mechanical Engineers*, started as a single journal in 1878, has expanded into 13 quarterly primary journals.

The growth of scientific journals has jeopardized their capacity to transmit information efficiently and rapidly. Scientists have to wade through a large mass of literature to keep themselves informed of current developments in their fields of specialization and in related peripheral fields.

B. Scattering of Journal Literature

Directly related to the problem of proliferation of journals is the phenomenon of scattering of articles on a given subject in a great many journals. Citation studies have established that in any given subject, a substantial proportion of the articles is concentrated in a relatively small number of journals, and the remaining articles are scattered in a very large number of journals peripheral to or outside the subject. This phenomenon of scattering of journal articles was first investigated by S.C. Bradford.[21,22] This has been followed by scores of citation analysis studies on the dispersion of literature in various disciplines.

Some degree of dispersion of articles in various journals may be desirable to promote cross-fertilization of ideas and serendipitous discoveries. But the disadvantages of the dispersion of papers in numerous journals have far outweighed the advantages of dispersion. The twin problems of proliferation of journals and dispersion of papers are of concern to authors, librarians, bibliographers, publishers of secondary services, and users of scientific literature. Editors of abstracting and indexing services and bibliographers have to scan large numbers of journals including those in fields peripheral or unrelated to their areas of interest to be reasonably sure of comprehensiveness. A typical scientist usually scans 6 to 8 journals regularly for current awareness. The effort of individual scientists to remain well informed of current developments in their fields of interest is always beset with the frightening possibility of their missing items that may be of crucial importance to their research.

C. Delay in Publication

Because of the elaborate editorial and refereeing processes, sometimes involving extensive and repeated revisions of the manuscript, the timelag between the submission of the first manuscript and the eventual publication of the paper in a journal may range from six months to a couple of years. The growing number of manuscripts that have to be processed also adds to the delay in publication. Garvey and coworkers have shown that, on the average, work reported in journal articles was begun 28 months prior to publication, was completed 15 months prior, and written up and submitted 8 months prior to publication.[23] Due to the delay inherent in the journal publication process, scientists resort to a variety of other channels to disseminate the results of their research; these include preprint distribution, conferences, and occasionally, the mass media of communication. Some scientists even resort to the unethical practice of submitting the same or substantially similar manuscripts to more than one journal at the same time.[24]

D. Diversity of Functions

The primary journal has been too general a package that has tried to be all things to all people, simultaneously attempting to fulfill many diverse functions:

1. An archival record of validated body of knowledge.
2. A current awareness tool for announcement of new discoveries.
3. An instrument through which scientists establish claims for priority to their contributions and build up their professional stature.
4. A book-reviewing medium to aid librarians in book selection.
5. A channel for the dissemination of a variety of commercial technical, personnel, and miscellaneous information.

Some of these roles are mutually incompatible. For example, the journal's role as an archival record necessitates thorough and time-consuming editing, refereeing and evaluation processes, whereas rapid publication (which may inhibit elaborate refereeing and editing) is indicated if the journal is to be an effective current awareness tool. In an attempt to perform such diverse, and sometimes mutually conflicting functions, the journal has not been very effective in any of these roles. According to Rossmassler, "the system does a good job of assembling knowledge into packages which are about 90 per cent mismatched to the needs of users."[25]

Also, because of the narrow specialization of scientists and the general nature of the journal, only a small proportion of the contents of a journal is useful to individual scientists.[26]

E. Increasing Costs

The journal is becoming increasingly more expensive. Publication costs are steadily going up, and so are subscription prices. The annual surveys of periodical prices reported in *Library Journal* each summer indicate that subscription prices of United States journals are increasing at rates of 10 to 13 per cent each year, and that chemistry and physics journals are the most expensive ones. The average price of chemistry and physics journals in 1982 was $177.94; this is nearly four times the average price of an American journal ($44.80) in 1982. The average prices of periodicals in several subject areas during 1981 and 1982 are shown in Table 1.

Data in Table 1 clearly indicate that periodicals in science, medicine, and engineering are more expensive than those in the social sciences and the humanities. Science and technology journals published by commercial publishers cost 5 to 15 times those published by learned societies.[28]

The problem of rising costs of journals is equally vexatious to scientists, librarians and publishers. The high price of scientific journals is rapidly removing the journal beyond the financial means of the individual scientist. The problem is further compounded by the dispersion of articles and the diverse nature of the contents of journals. A scientist subscribing to a journal is forced to pay for 15 or 20 papers in each issue which do not concern him, in order to get the two or three that are of interest.

The impact on libraries is equally ravaging. Libraries have been attempting to meet this situation in a variety of ways, among which are: transferring book budgets to serials, cooperative acquisition, participation in networks for resource sharing, and, when inevitable, cancellation of subscriptions to journals.

Editorial and composition costs, which constitute a substantial part of the total cost of journal production, have also been increasing. Journal publishers have responded by (a) increasing subscription rates, (b) charging higher subscription rates to libraries than to individual subscribers, (c) eliminating discounts allowed to subscription agents, and (d) asking for page charges or publication charges.

The concept of page charges was pioneered by the American Institute of Physics, and subsequently endorsed by the U. S. Federal Council for Science and Technology and also in the SATCOM Report.[29-31] Although page charges are said to be voluntary, it is suspected that some societies give a higher priority in their publication schedule to papers covered by page charges over those not so covered, thus bringing indirect pressure on contributors (or their employers or sponsors) to pay page charges. For articles to be published in the *Reviews of Geophysics and Space Physics,* the Ameri-

Table 1. Survey of Periodical Prices [27]

Subject	Average price 1982 $	Average price 1981 $	Percentage increase
Chemistry and physics	177.94	156.30	13.85
Medicine	102.87	86.38	19.09
Mathematics, botany, geology, and general science	87.99	75.62	16.36
Engineering	61.54	54.55	13.36
Zoology	61.07	48.32	26.39
Psychology	54.21	47.27	14.68
Sociology and anthropology	36.38	31.37	15.97
Home economics	34.27	27.34	25.35
Journalism and communications	33.91	29.80	11.38
Library science	33.52	28.47	17.74
Business and economics	32.67	28.88	13.12
Education	28.18	25.18	11.91
Law	27.53	24.80	11.00
Industrial arts	27.13	22.62	19.94
Political science	25.89	22.69	14.10
Labor and industrial relations	24.72	21.68	14.02
General interest periodicals	23.93	21.83	9.62
Fine and applied arts	23.35	20.51	13.85
History	20.37	17.96	13.42
Agriculture	19.76	17.24	14.62
Literature and language	19.39	17.30	12.08
Philosophy and religion	17.92	15.40	16.36
Physical education and recreation	16.91	15.42	9.66
Children's periodicals	9.90	8.56	15.65
United States periodicals	44.80	39.13	14.49

can Geophysical Union asks for publication charges of $81 per page if the articles have to be typeset by the publisher, and $42 per page if the author provides camera-ready copy. For papers to be published in *Water Resources Research,* the page charge is $125 per page. In either case, authors paying publication charges or page charges receive 100 reprints without further charges.

Many journal publishers have dual subscription rates; in recent years, subscription rates for libraries have increased more steeply than rates for individual subscribers. A survey of dual pricing practices among publishers of health-related journals identified 281 periodicals with an average price differential of over 100 per cent between individual and institutional subscription rates. Both the dual pricing practice itself and the amount of the differential were found to be increasing. "Uncritical purchasing" of journals by libraries seems to underwrite, at least partly, the increasing costs of journal publishing.[32]

V. CURRENT TRENDS IN JOURNAL PUBLISHING

Several innovations have been suggested and tried with varying degrees of success to offset the problems discussed in the preceding sections. Some of these are simple modifications that can be incorporated into the existing structure of the journal to improve the speed of dissemination of scientific information. Other suggestions have been more drastic. The following are some of the measures currently being tried to improve the speed and economics of journal publishing.

A. Computer-Aided Production

Modern methods of composition and printing, increasingly aided by the computer, have considerably speeded up journal publication. Letterpress printing is rendered obsolete by the faster and more economic offset process. Traditional methods of composition are being replaced by computerized photocomposition, COM (computer output microform), and composition using a wide variety of word-processing equipment. The advent of COM has greatly speeded up the production of both microfilm and offset master directly from the computer, thus eliminating many time-consuming intermediate steps in the preparation of the offset master. The impact of computer and communication technologies on journal publishing will be discussed in detail in a later section.

B. Auxiliary Publication

Another solution to the problems of the growing volume of published material and the delay in its publication has been to print only the main text of the paper in the journal and to store all auxiliary material (such as supporting data, computer programs, mathematical derivations, bibliographies) on microfilm or microfiche in a depository for dissemination to users in response to specific requests. The National Auxiliary Publication Service of the American Society for Information Science is an example of this trend. The American Chemical Society, the American Psychological Association, the British Library Lending Division, and the Canadian Research Council are among other organizations that have similar provision for storage of auxiliary material.

In the *Journal of Biological Chemistry,* supporting material is printed separately as a "miniprint" section directly from photoreduction of typed·pages supplied by the author. The miniprint section can be read with the help of a standard magnifying glass. A footnote in the paper containing a miniprint section indicates the cost and procedure for obtaining full-size photocopies of the original typed pages. In addition, the Materials and Methods section of all papers in that journal are printed in a somewhat smaller type than that used for the rest of the paper.

C. Microform Publication

Several journal publishers such as the American Chemical Society, the American Institute of Physics, the Institute of Electrical and Electronics Engineers, and the American Medical Association, have resorted to microform publication in addition to the publication of printed copies of their journals. Journals on microfiche can be mailed first class, and reach the user faster than paper editions. Although microform editions are compact, portable, and usually cheaper than paper editions, user acceptance of microforms has been slow. Gannett has reported a survey in which only one per cent of the members of the Society of Automotive Engineers and the IEEE preferred microfiche to the printed edition.[33] The University Microfilms International offers about 13,000 serials (including journals and newspapers) on microfilm and microfiche. The company also supplies the necessary equipment and furniture.

D. "Letters" Journals

A new type of journal known as short communication journal or "letters" journal, has come into existence exclusively for the rapid publication of preliminary findings of research. The articles published in such journals are usually short, and receive minimal or no editing. Some letters journals (e.g., *Tetrahedron Letters*) use the author's copy for printing, thus considerably speeding up the production process. The timelag of publication in *Chemical Physics Letters* is said to be 14 days from the date of acceptance of the manuscript.[34] *Tetrahedron Letters* attempts to publish communications within four weeks. *Radiochemical and Radioanalytical Letters* publishes short articles (maximum length 1,500 words) within eight weeks from the date of receipt of the manuscript.

In a comparative study of *Analytical Chemistry* and *Analytical Letters,* the mean timelags were found to be 191 days and 33 days respectively.[35] This timelag represented the interval between the receipt of the manuscript in the editorial office and the actual distribution of the printed journals.

E. The Synopsis Journal

The idea of publishing scientific papers at two levels of completeness was proposed at the Royal Society Scientific Information Conference by Pirie, and later by Bernal and Phipps.[36-38] This suggestion was based on the premise that a majority of journal users are interested in the general outlines and conclusions of a research paper, and only a small proportion of readers are interested in a detailed account of the research project. In 1968, the American Chemical Society examined a proposal to publish its *Journal of Organic Chemistry* in two editions: A complete edition with full experimental data and details for libraries, and a condensed version with only the main findings and limited data for general circulation. A survey of subscribers' reaction to this proposal led to the conclusion that "such a system, while perhaps needed, could not unilaterally be adopted by the *Journal of Organic Chemistry* without loss in favor."[39] In another experiment in 1976, the American Chemical Society published the *Journal of the American Chemical Society* in two editions: (a) A summary version, containing synopses of research papers, prepared by the authors themselves. This version, primarily intended for individual subscribers, also contained book reviews and communications to the editor. (b) An archival edition, primarily meant for libraries, contained reproduction of the authors' typewritten manuscript at a reduced size. A survey of authors, reviewers, editors, librarians, and readers showed that "although no 'mandate' was evident for conversion of *JACS* to a dual journal, strong evidence was obtained of an interest in, and need for, summary journals."[40] Several other similar experiments have been conducted to study the economics and acceptability of synopsis journals.[41-44]

VI. FUTURE PROSPECTS: THE ELECTRONIC JOURNAL

The most important single force that is sure to influence the basic structure of the primary journal is the electronic computer. Several journal publishers such as the American Chemical Society and the American Institute of Physics have developed computer-based techniques for keyboarding manuscripts, typesetting, microform publication through COM, and for index production.[45-50] But the computer has not so far altered the basic structure of the primary journal; it has been used simply to expedite certain operations (e.g., typesetting) that were being earlier performed manually or by electromechanical means. However, in the not too distant future, the printed journal may be rendered obsolete, or at least partially replaced, by a distributed computer network that would facilitate intercontinental interactive communication among various groups of users including authors, editors, referees, information analysts, and scientist-users.[51-56] In addition to performing, in an online mode, the basic functions of manuscript input, reviewing and editing, and housekeeping operations, such an "electronic journal" system would provide an extended spectrum of services such as browsing facility, retrospective searching, commentaries, user scratchpads and filing systems, and data manipulation capability. It would be possible for the user, for example, to manipulate the data presented in a paper, draw graphs, and have the results of computations displayed on the terminal. The user would be able to communicate with other users over the network through computer conferencing. Authors in different geographical areas could collaborate in preparing articles. The electronic journal could also carry news items and even advertisements.

Besides being faster than the traditional printed journal, the electronic journal can provide international access to scientific papers in an online mode, can capture "fugitive materials" such as unpublished technical reports, and is also expected to be more cost-effective than an equivalently large paper journal.[57] The National Science Foundation has sponsored a series of experimental projects to study the feasibility and acceptability of the electronic journal. At the New Jersey Institute of Technology, the Electronic Information Exchange System has supported the development of four different forms of electronic journal. In a progress report on this project, Turoff and Hiltz wrote in 1982: "We are at least a decade away from substantially supplementing print-based journals with electronic ones, but the first [experimental prototype] electronic journals are here."[58]

A similar experimental electronic journal on mental workload has been reported by Sheridan et al.[59] In England, the British Library Research and Development Department has sponsored an electronic journal entitled *Computer Human Factors*.[60]

In spite of its futuristic appeal and advantages in terms of speed, flexibility, and economy, the electronic journal is not without its share of drawbacks and impediments. Political and social factors tend, in general, to retard any drastic change in the journal system.[61] Turoff and Hiltz feel that there are human problems, some lingering technological problems, and policy problems including those relating to international data transmission.[62] User acceptance can be slow. "Terminals cannot be carried into the subway or to bed; nor are they 'cuddly.' But neither were the first books which were chained to library walls and shelves to prevent theft."[63] Though miniaturization can soon produce portable terminals, Senders feels that "perhaps users' acceptance will have to await the retrenchment of the older scientists."[64]

The electronic journal will become widely available in the not too distant future. With it, our perceptions of "journal," "paper," and "publishing" will also have to change. A paper printed in the traditional journal is a fixed entity frozen in time; but a paper "published" in an electronic journal is a dynamic entity that can change at any time and any number of times, based on feedback from readers and the author's reaction to such feedback. Even at the present time, the current status of publishing technology allows papers to be delivered in a variety of media: Microfilm, microfiche, microprint, diskette, audio/videotape, computer tape, and loose-leaf; it can also be delivered "on-demand." When the electronic journal makes available online access to papers, the printed scientific journal will no longer be the only medium for the dissemination of current information or for the archival preservation of the recorded knowledge of science; it will have to compete and coexist with its electronic counterpart.

REFERENCES

1. Harrod, Leonard M. *The librarian's glossary of terms used in librarianship, documentation and the book crafts and reference book.* 4th ed. Boulder: Westview Press; 1977: p. 633.
2. Machlup, Fritz; Leeson, Kenneth. *Information through the printed word. the dissemination of scholarly, scientific, and intellectual knowledge.* vol. 2: Journals. New York: Praeger Publishers; 1978.
3. Machlup, et al., *op.cit.*
4. Porter, J. R. The scientific journal—300th anniversary. *Bacteriological Reviews.* 28(3): 215-216; 1964 September.
5. Kronick, David A. *A history of scientific and technical periodicals. The origins and development of the scientific and technical press, 1665-1790.* 2d ed. Metuchen: Scarecrow Press; 1976.
6. McKie, Douglas. The scientific periodical from 1665 to 1798. *Philosophical Magazine.* 122-132; 1948. Reprinted in: Meadows, A. J. *The scientific journal.* London: Aslib; 1979: p. 7-17.
7. A debate on preprint exchange. *Physics Today.* 19:60-73; 1966 June.
8. Subramanyam, K. Information exchange groups: An experiment in science communication. *Indian Librarian.* 29(4):159-164; 1975 March.
9. Brown, W. S.; Pierce, J. R.; Traub, J. F. The future of scientific journals. *Science.* 158(3805):1153-1159; 1967 Dec. 1.
10. Carroll, Kenneth D. Development of a national information system for physics. *Special Libraries.* 61:171-179; 1970 April.
11. Phelps, Ralph H. Alternatives to the scientific periodical: a report and bibliography. *Unesco Bulletin for Libraries.* 14(2):61-75; 1960.
12. Hills, Jacqueline. *Review of the literature on primary communication in science and technology.* London: Aslib; 1972.
13. Subramanyam, K. *Scientific and technical information resources.* New York: Marcel Dekker; 1981: p. 47-51.
14. Herschman, Arthur. The primary journal: past, present, and future. *Journal of Chemical Documentation.* 10(1):37-42; 1970 February.
15. Gottschalk, Charles M.; Desmond, Winifred F. World-wide census of scientific and technical serials. *American Documentation.* 14(3):188-194; 1963 July.
16. Brown, Charles H. *Scientific serials: Characteristics and lists of most cited publications in mathematics, physics, chemistry, geology, physiology, botany, zoology and entomology.* (ACRL monograph No. 16). Chicago: Association of College and Research Libraries; 1956.
17. Purpose in publication. *Nature.* 191(4788):527-530; 1961. Aug. 5.
18. Mangla, P. B. Scientific literature and documentation. *Herald of Library Science.* 3(4):286-292; 1964 October.

19. Barr, K. P. Estimates of the number of currently available scientific and technical periodicals. *Journal of Documentation.* 23(2):110-116; 1967.

20. King. Donald W. and others. *Scientific journals in the United States: their production, use, and economics.* Stroudsburg, Pa.: Hutchinson Ross Publishing Co.; 1981: p. 23-26.

21. Bradford, S. C. On the scattering of scientific subjects in scientific periodicals. *Engineering.* 137:85-86; 1934.

22. Bradford, S. C. *Documentation.* 2d ed. London: Crosby Lockwood; 1953. p. 18.

23. Garvey, William D. and others. Some comparisons of communication activities in the physical and social sciences. *In: Communication among scientists and engineers,* ed. by Nelson, Carnot E. and Pollock, Donald K. Lexington, Mass.: D. C. Heath & Co.; 197?: p. 63.

24. Abelson, Philip H. Excessive zeal to publish. *Science.* 218(4576): 593; 3 December 1982. See also correspondence, "Duplicate publication," *Science.* 219(4588):1020-1022; 1983 March 4.

25. Rossmassler, Stephan A. Scientific literature in policy decision making. *Journal of Chemical Documentation.* 10:163-167; 1970 August.

26. Kuney, Joseph A.; Weissgerber, William H. System requirements for primary journal systems: utilization of the *Journal of Organic Chemistry. Journal of Chemical Documentation.* 10:150-157; 1970 August.

27. Brown, Norman B. and Phillips, Jane. Price indexes for 1982: U.S. periodicals and serial services. *Library Journal.* 107(14):1379-1382; 1982 August.

28. Moore, James A. An inquiry on new forms of primary publications. *Journal of Chemical Documentation.* 12:75-78; 1972 May.

29. Barton, H. A. The publication charge plan in physics journals. *Physics Today.* 16:45-47; 1963 June.

30. Koch, H. William. Publication charges and financial solvency. *Physics Today.* 21:126-127; 1968 December.

31. *Scientific and technical communication. A pressing national problem and recommendations for its solution.* Washington, D.C.: National Academy of Sciences, 1969: p. 66, 121.

32. Miller, Dick R.; Jensen, Joseph E. Dual pricing of health sciences periodicals: a survey. *Bulletin of the Medical Library Association.* 68(4): 336-340; 1980 October.

33. Gannett, Elwood K. Primary publication systems and services. *Annual Review of Information Science and Technology.* 8:261; 1973.

34. Grogan, Denis J. *Science and technology: An introduction to the literature.* 3d ed. London: Clive Bingley; 1976: p. 157.

35. Subramanyam, K.; Schaffer, Constance J. Effectiveness of "letters" journals. *New Library World.* 75:258-259; 1974 December.

36. Pirie, N. W. Note on the simultaneous publication of papers at two different levels of completeness. *In: The Royal Society Scientific Information Conference, 21 June - 2 July 1948. Report and Papers Submitted.* London: The Royal Society; 1948: p. 419-422.

37. Bernal, J. D. The transmission of scientific information: a user's analysis. *In: Proceedings of the International Conference on Scientific Information, 1958.* Washington, D.C.: National Academy of Sciences, National Research Council; 1959; vol. 1 (p. 77-95).

38. Phipps, T. E. Scientific communication. *Science.* 129(3342): 118; 1959 January 16.

39. Moore, *op cit.*

40. Terrant, Seldon W.; Garson, Lorrin R. Evaluation of a dual journal concept. *Journal of Chemical Information and Computer Sciences.* 17(2): 61-67; 1977 May.

41. Barlow, D. H. A & I services as database producers: economic, technological and cooperative opportunities. *Aslib Proceedings.* 28(10): 325-337; 1976 October.

42. Rowland, J. F. B. Synopsis journals as seen by their authors. *Journal of Documentation.* 37(2):69-76; 1981 June.

43. Manten, Arie A. Possible future relevance of publishing scholarly information in the form of synopses. *Journal of Information Science.* 1(5): 293-296; 1980 January.

44. Dutta, S. Synopsis journals—communication media for a transition period. *Annals of Library Science and Documentation.* 29(2):45-50; 1982.

45. Kuney, Joseph. New developments in primary journal publication. *Journal of Chemical Documentation.* 10:42-46; 1970 February.

46. Herschman, Arthur. Keeping up with what's going on in physics. *Physics Today.* 24:23-29; 1971 November.

47. Metzner, A. W. Kenneth. Multiple use and other benefits of computerized publishing. *IEEE Transactions on Professional Communication.* PC-18(3):274-278; 1975 September.

48. Parisi, Paul A. Composition innovations at the ASCE. *IEEE Transactions on Professional Communication.* PC-18(3):244-273; 1975 September.

49. Bemer, Robert W.; Shriver, A. Richard. Integrating computer text processing with photocomposition. *IEEE Transactions on Professional Communication.* PC-16(3):92-96; 1973 September.

50. Korbuly, Dorothy K. A new approach to coding displayed mathematics for photocomposition. *IEEE Transactions on Professional Communication.* PC-18(3):283-287; 1975 September.

51. Bamford, Harold. A concept for applying computer technology to the publication of scientific journals. *Journal of the Washington Academy of Science.* 62:306-314; 1972.

52. Bamford, Harold. The editorial processing center. *IEEE Transactions on Professional Communication.* PC-16(3):82-83; 1973 September.

53. Rhodes, Sarah N.; Bamford, Harold E. Editorial processing centers: A progress report. *American Sociologist.* 11:153-159; 1976 August.

54. *Editorial processing centers: feasibility and promise.* Rockville, Md.: Aspen Systems Corporation; Westat, Inc.; 1976.

55. Senders, J. W.; Anderson, C. M. B.; Hecht, C. D. *Scientific publication systems: an analysis of past, present and future methods of scientific communication.* Springfield, Va.: National Technical Information Service; 1975 June; PB242259.

56. Senders, John W. The scientific journal of the future. *The American Sociologist.* 11:160-164; 1976.

57. Herschman, The primary journal, *op cit.*

58. Turoff, Murray; Hiltz, Starr Roxanne. The electronic journal: A progress report. *Journal of the American Society for Information Science.* 33(4):195-202; 1982 July.

59. Sheridan, R.; Senders, J.; Moray, N.; Stoklosa, J.; Guillaume, J.; Makepeace, D. *Experimentation with a multi-disciplinary teleconference and electronic journal on mental workload.* Report to the National Science Foundation, Division of Science Information Access Improvement. 320p.

60. Shackel, B. The BLEND system: Programme for the study of some electronic journals. *Journal of the American Society for Information Science.* 34(1):22-30; 1983 January.

61. Cawkell, A. E. Electronic information processing and publishing: problems and opportunities. *Journal of the American Society for Information Science.* 2(3/4):189-192; 1982 October.

62. Turoff & Hiltz, *op cit.*

63. Raben, Joseph. The electronic revolution and the world just around the corner. *Scholarly Publishing.* 10(3):195-209; 1979 April.

64. Senders, J. An online scientific journal. *The Information Scientist.* 11(1):3-9; 1977.

A Computer-Based Routing System for Serials

Rita L. Goodemote

ABSTRACT. The routing of journals as a means of disseminating information has been a function of the Schering Corporation library since its inception. The original concept of convenience to the user expanded to that of necessity as decentralization increased and multi-New Jersey locations had to be served. The inability of manual systems employed to permit additions, deletions, address changes, and a logical flow of material created a demand for a more flexible method. A computer-based routing system provided the solution.

In a pharmaceutical corporate situation, where research is the lifeline to the future of the corporation, exposure to appropriate literature is an essential part of the research process. But for the busy scientist, spending hours in the library reviewing current journals is a luxury that few have the time to indulge.

Routing publications is one assured way of disseminating information to those who need it. This not only provides exposure to specific articles which might be identified from a table of contents service, but there is an additional bonus which results from browsing. As proponents of this viewpoint, we make journals available to all personnel through our routing system, regardless of their proximity to library copies, and without imposing a numerical limitation.

The case for not routing journals may have some validity in organizations where operations are centralized at a single location. The more decentralization that occurs, the greater the need for reaching personnel at all sites. Satellite libraries offer a partial solution, but some routing is still unavoidable. A single geographic site is not the situation at Schering-Plough, nor has it ever been during my tenure.

We found maintaining viable route lists manually to be virtually

---

Rita L. Goodemote is Associate Director, Library Information Center, Pharmaceutical Research Division, Schering-Plough Corporation, 60 Orange Street, Bloomfield, NJ 07003.

© 1983 by The Haworth Press, Inc. All rights reserved.

impossible. Frequent additions, deletions, and location changes required almost constant updating. The enthusiasm engendered by our adopting the VISIRecord method of posting journal receipt and generating route slips some years ago soon faded. The realization came that changes on the hectograph master, while easier to make, still resulted in an irrational movement of the publications when the individual inserted in the space vacated by a deletion was located at a different site.

As the number of routees and locations increased, it became evident that a computer-based system was needed to provide more flexibility and a greater degree of currency.

We reviewed what other organizations had worked out, and then turned to our Computer and Information Science department with an outline of what we expected to accomplish and to solicit their assistance with the required programming.

PLANNING

The establishment of objectives was the first item to be identified. We determined that the main purpose of the system was to be the provision of computer-produced routing slips to be attached to journals circulated on a regular basis.

The lists were to contain the title of the journal, its copy number, the names of routees with their company locations, and the final destination of the journal—Library Information Center (LIC) or its Chemical Library satellite, Bloomfield, or Business Information Center (BIC), Kenilworth.

A requirement was that the system developed had to eliminate the large amount of clerical effort involved in the manual preparation of route lists by providing an easy updating method for all information in the system, and convenient user indexes for referencing this information. The assigned programmer set about providing such a system.

DATA PREPARATION

Preparation of the input was the task of the LIC staff. Detailed information on journals and routees was gathered as the first step.

An alphabetical list of journal titles was coded, using an alphanumeric code comprised of the first letter of the journal title followed by four digits, spaced adequately to accommodate insertion of new titles. Frequency of publication, circulating and non-circulating copies available, and identification of the collection location of these copies (LIC, BIC, or Chemical Library) was part of the journal profile.

Simultaneously, a routee file was prepared. The basis for this was the existing manual file. For each individual, employee number, expense center and company location were determined. These were verified by the individuals at the start-up of the system.

Finally an assignment file was created by combining routees with journal titles received.

Establishing the best routing path presented a problem. The original concept of priority by location proved to be impractical, since all journals would follow the same pattern regardless of subject matter. It was decided to vary the path based on a list of 26 broad categories, e.g., Medicine, Chemistry, Microbiology/Virology, Marketing, International, etc. Priority by location was then determined on the premise of need to be kept informed in particular subject areas. For each location, names were ordered alphabetically. Exceptional needs were satisfied by individual priorities, which would override all other arrangements.

Computer-stored dictionaries, to be consulted in formatting route lists, were compiled for Expense Centers, Locations, Address Priorities, Journal Categories, and Publication Frequencies.

SYSTEM DESIGN

While we were engaged in gathering data for input, our programmer was developing the data entry formats. The design for each format is described.

1. Journal information input required two punched cards.
   a. Card 1 contained
      Type of transaction (new record, correction record or deletion record)
      Record type and number (J01)
      Journal code
      Journal title
   b. Card 2 (J02) repeated transaction type and journal code and added:

Frequency of publication code
   Number of circulating copies at 3 locations
   Number of non-circulating copies at 3 locations
   Publication type (if abstract or index)
   Journal category
2. Routee input format involved transaction type, record type and number (R01) plus:
   Routee code (employee number)
   Expense Center
   Company address
   Routee name
3. Assignment input format gave transaction type, record type and number (A01) plus:
   Journal code
   Routee code
   Personal priority code for title
4. Card format for expense center input required transaction type, record type and number (D01) plus:
   Expense Center number
   Expense Center name
5. Priorities by address input was the most difficult one to set up, since it involved identifying the needs of staff at each location (site, building and floor) for early receipt of specific categories of information.

It was based on the assumption that individuals at the same location have essentially the same priority rights. And unfortunately, it is judgmental.

For example, it was assumed that the address housing the International division should have first priority for journals concerned with international business, as well as high priority for management, marketing, finance, general business, drug trade. Some populations at other locations and their needs could not be as clearly defined.

REPORTS

In addition to the production of routing slips, the system was designed to generate a series of lists and reports which would serve as reference points. Lists were produced for Locations (Bloomfield, Kenilworth, Union, etc.), Routees (arranged alphabetically by name and numerically by employee number), Expense Centers (numerically arranged with descriptive names of centers), Address priorities (for each address), Assignments (list of journal codes followed by employee numbers, with individual priorities indicated).

Reports generated consisted of:

1. Routee/Journal Report – routees arranged alphabetically with indication of all journals being routed.
2. Journal/Routee Report – journal titles, with routees for each copy of journal. This is a continuous run which is a duplicate of individually printed route lists.
3. Journal/Routee Summary Report – journal name and code, total number of routees per title, number of routees per copy.

ADDITIONAL CAPABILITIES

The system was programmed to provide additional information—journal holdings data for each library. This was never implemented, and possibly will not be in the future. Development of serial control systems has opened up another approach to recording holdings information.

FORMS

Preparatory to initiation of the system, specifications for forms that would be needed had to be determined.

Specifications for routing list paper were submitted to Forms Control. Paper 11" wide and 7" long, with adhesive strips running the length of the left and right margins was requisitioned. Two route lists per page were planned, making for 5 1/2" × 7" forms following bursting at perforations.

Another requirement was designing an easy-to-use form for new routees, current routees wanting to add or delete titles, or current routees who transferred to new locations or expense centers.

The resulting form permitted direct keypunching following verification of journal codes used, routee status, and expense center validity.

A form memo was also designed to send to individuals requesting routing of non-circulating titles, those not subscribed to, or those which have ceased publication or have been cancelled.

SYSTEM START-UP

For the initial input to start up the system, keypunch sheets were filled in for journals, routees, assignments, expense centers and names, locations, and address priorities, using the designated formats. Keypunching was done in the Computer and Information department and computer runs, as well as the route list printing, were carried out by our staff.

The elapsed time between the design of the system and its implementation was almost two years. Staffing problems, with attendant inability to commit total effort to the input project, were responsible. The first computer-based route lists went into effect in July 1976.

FILE UPDATE

All lists, reports, and routing slips are updated monthly, effecting reasonable currency. Situations which require updating are:

— Addition of new routee with his assignments
— Addition of journal assignments of current routee
— Termination of routee with his assignments
— Deletion of journal assignments of current routee
— Transfer of routee to new location and/or expense center
— Establishment of personal priority for current routee
— Addition of new journal title
— Deletion of journal title
— Journal title change
— Journal frequency change
— Change in number of copies received
— Change in circulating (or non-circulating) status
— Change in file location

The routing request forms, spoken of earlier, usually serve for input covering routee and assignment information. Changes are also picked up from a weekly Personnel report listing new employees, terminations, and home address changes. Since company address changes are not shown here unless they involve transfer between divisions, it is sometimes difficult to keep pace with these changes.

Journal information modifications are input on IBM keypunching sheets, since this type of information is acquired internally and not from the requester.

PERIODIC REVIEW

The routing situation is reviewed biannually. The large amount of staff effort required to effect major changes which result precludes more frequent reviews. It is assumed also that individuals will generally take the initiative in modifying their reading patterns if their roles change significantly.

When reviews are carried out, each individual receives a computer-generated list of the journals currently received accompanied by a list of the journals available for routing. An attached memo requests that all changes be entered on the Routing Request Forms to expedite the input process.

SYSTEM MAINTENANCE

The updating activity, involving input, keypunching, card reading, report generation, verification procedures, route list generation, bursting, collation and route list filing requires two to two-and-a half staff days per month.

After the initial data entry, all subsequent activities are initiated by use of an interactive terminal. Data correction is accomplished by interactive editing.

Computer costs are low, running between $10 and $15 per month. There is no documentation regarding machine and personnel costs to start up the routing system.

Some current statistics: out of approximately 1000 journal titles received in the LIC for the three libraries, 725 titles (1100 copies) are routed to 1500 individuals in New Jersey.

PROGRAM AND EQUIPMENT

The computer program for the routing system was written in COBOL. The system utilizes a Digital Equipment Card Reader and DECwriter III, IBM R370, model 3033 under MVS, PDP 11/70, Data Products Printer, model B600 and Advanced Terminals Inc. Formstaker.

SYSTEM EVALUATION

The chief advantage of the system is its updating feature. It is simple to maintain, and allows for centralization within the LIC of all activities except keypunching and bursting. In addition, it is economical and demands only about 25% of the staff time that was required for all the previously tried manual systems.

The updated lists generated each month serve as reference sources which are frequently consulted for activities relevant to and apart from the routing system.

The Journal/Routee Summary Report is an indicator of journal usage. Since it reports the total number of routees per title and the number on each copy, it signals the point at which an additional copy must be procured or another alternative taken (changing status of non-circulating copy or attempting to convince some routees to consult the library copy). The system accepts twenty-five routees per copy, which is reasonable for newsy publications, but too many for medical and technical journals. Budgetary considerations dictate the number of multiples that can be subscribed.

One deficiency of the system is its inability to readily identify claims to be made for nonreceipt of issues. Route slips for each circulating title are generated each month, even for bimonthly, quarterly and irregular titles. The route slips remaining at the end of each month do not necessarily represent issues to be claimed. The posting record has to be perused to establish this. The rationale for programming this way was the inability to predict receipt dates.

We are satisfied with the performance of our computer-based routing system, and have elected not to abandon it in favor of systems that may have more sophistication. It has served well for almost seven years with only a few minor modifications.

Unfortunately, routees cannot be programmed to pass publications along expeditiously in spite of the message on each route slip to "Read and pass quickly." Individual, location, or alphabetical priorities are the only assurances of early receipt of a circulating journal.

REFERENCES

The following references were consulted prior to designing our routing system:

Blair, Joan. Routing slips from the computer. *Special Libraries.* 63(2): 82-84; 1972 February.

Collins, Kenneth Alan; West, William W. Data management systems. Part II. Journal routing - an example of library applications. *Special Libraries.* 65(4):205-211; 1975 April.

Feldman, Myra S.; Maddox, Judith H. *A computer program for circulation and control of library journals.* Aiken, S.C.: E.I. DuPont de Nemours and Company; 1969 January.

Jones, H.W. Computerized subscription and periodicals routing in an aerospace library. *Special Libraries.* 58(11):634-638; 1967 November.

Riggle, Stella-Margaret. Automatic journal routing using IBM punched cards. *Special Libraries.* 53(11):537-540; 1962 November.

Stevenson, Chris G. An inexpensive computer-based system for group routing periodicals. *Special Libraries.* 61(10):460-470; 1970 October.

Yerkey, A. Neil. Computer-assisted periodical routing and renewal audit. *Special Libraries.* 64(3):126-129; 1973 March.

Young, Barbara A. Computer-generated routing slips. *Special Libraries.* 65(2):68-73; 1975 February.

Choosing and Using Subscription Agents in Sci-Tech Libraries: Theory and Practice

Sheila S. Intner

ABSTRACT. Explores the controversy about the value of using subscription agents as found in the library literature in view of the special needs of sci-tech libraries for serials/periodicals and current problems in their acquisitions. Surveys several sci-tech libraries to learn their current practices and priorities in using agents for their serial/periodical acquisitions.

From time to time we find articles in the literature about the value, or lack of it, in using subscription agents to acquire periodicals and other serial publications. Katz and Gellatly, noted authorities on all aspects of serial librarianship, suggest as a rule of thumb that a library should use a subscription agent if they receive more than one hundred titles, even if the agent charges them up to 20% in service fees.[1] Quite the opposite, Huibert Paul, serials librarian at the University of Oregon library, charges, "subscription agents do not save university libraries work. Nor do they save us money."[2] Who is correct? On what do they base their differing opinions? What are sci-tech librarians deciding for their own operations? What criteria should influence their decisions?

To answer the questions posed above, we will examine arguments posed in the literature by those who favor and oppose use of subscription agents; and then investigate the practices of several science and technology librarians in the field by means of an informal research study.

Sheila S. Intner is Assistant Professor at the School of Library Service of Columbia University, and teaches courses in technical services. She received her BA in Economics and Political Science from Northwestern University, MLS from Queens College of the City University of New York, and a DLS from Columbia University.

© 1983 by The Haworth Press, Inc. All rights reserved.

Huff names the following functions of a subscription agent:[3]

1. To act as a single source for publications from many publishers;
2. To provide standard invoicing; and
3. To give service, not materials, by accurate and prompt placing of new orders; speedy and vigorous claiming; timely renewals of expiring subscriptions; and bibliographic assistance.

According to Huff, librarians value agents not for their ability to provide materials, but for their services, especially in the areas of finance, the management of many accounts, and the speed with which they attend to the necessary adjustments of claiming, renewal, reimbursement for journals that cease publication, etc. Reliability counts for a great deal, and willingness to go under bond and/or furnish references are ways agents can prove their dependability and honesty.

The unspoken assumption is that if a library receives many serial publications, librarians and their staffs cannot perform the complex tasks of managing them as well as subscription agents; and even if they can, it will cost them more than the fees charged by the agents.

It may be useful to review the claims made by agents themselves, although Huff warns that advertising claims are sometimes "optimistic."[4] EBSCO, which together with Faxon accounts for the lion's share of the subscription market, promises "to enter subscriptions, service delivery and, *if necessary and possible,* obtain substitution or refund."[5] That entirely reasonable promise doesn't say anything about doing the job faster, more cheaply, or more effectively than the librarian. While disclaiming responsibility for "governmental mails or final delivery"[6] they promise to be responsive and flexible and give personalized service.[7] They claim to use their database of serial titles to supply all serials needs and information, foreign and domestic.[8] Though Paul says that publishers' current policies indicate they no longer value the services of agents, EBSCO claims to represent over 47,000 publishers.[9] This representation appears to be more in the nature of communicating with them—natural for an agent in the course of placing orders, paying bills, and managing libraries' subscriptions—rather than being designated representatives by publishers.

Literature from the Turner Agency claims to provide "an efficient, economic . . . service."[10] In 1981, EBSCO had a database of

140,000 titles while Turner claimed access to 60,000. Two years later, Turner increased this number to 150,000, and presumably, EBSCO's access increased similarly. Turner literature emphasizes its pre-payment on the client's behalf for speedy response from publishers.

Agents' literature offers several services to clients:[11]

1. Information—obviously, timely and accurate information on foreign and domestic titles is of value; alternative sources for title verification and availability would have to be supplied by the library if they were not provided by the agent; however, the burden of correctly identifying titles for purchase rests with the library—both Turner and EBSCO are crystal clear about this.
2. Consolidated billing and accounting—more valuable to libraries subscribing to larger numbers of titles involving a full range of idiosyncratic publication patterns, this service appeals to everyone whose common sense directs that paying one bill must be more economical than paying a hundred or more separate bills.
3. Follow-up services—here is an area where time-consuming and, therefore, costly letter-writing or phoning to make claims for lost issues, request adjustments or refunds for issues that will never arrive because of publisher error or default, or cancel unwanted subscriptions, is avoided on the part of the librarian, especially if (s)he might be expected to handle all this in addition to a full range of other duties.

Beyond these three categories of service, no concrete promises are made. Comparing them to Huff's three functions of an agent, they coincide quite well.

Now let us examine the arguments of an expert who is less sanguine about the value of subscription agents. Huibert Paul believes that the discounts publishers gave to agents years ago were the means whereby agents could afford to sell their services to libraries for what seemed to be less than nothing. In those days, in addition to receiving services, librarians often paid less for their serials than if they had dealt directly with publishers.[12] Today, however, the picture has changed in two respects. First, publishers now appear to be wooing the library customer at the expense of the middleperson, giving everyone the same treatment, or cutting the dealer's discount down to almost nothing. Since the agent is in business to make a profit, however small, the cost of doing business has to be paid by the client if it is not covered by the subscription discount. Second, newer techniques of disseminating information on the part of the publishers confound the agents' ability to save their clients paperwork—the time and trouble of attending to publishers' mailings, multiple billings, and so forth. Paul identifies three kinds of paperwork for libraries caused by these new developments:[13]

1. Publishers no longer inform agents in advance of price changes, so agents have to make many billing adjustments. Two of the librarians participating in the research survey mentioned this as a problem.
2. Direct mailings to all customers from computerized lists means libraries are peppered with announcements, invoices, etc., each of which has to be searched if the library, like most, orders some titles directly from publishers and others from agents.
3. Handling this unwanted "junk mail" often leads librarians to discover special rates, multi-year renewals at better prices and other advantages offered by publishers that agents have not relayed to them, but that may require a direct response. This was one of the chief complaints of one of the librarians in the survey.

Changes which have occurred over the years have led to problems for subscription agents. The most serious is the willingness of publishers to deal with individual subscribers on more-or-less the same basis as agents, once considered the professional subscribers and, thus, entitled to special treatment. Automation of publishers' mailing lists makes it uneconomic for them to distinguish between direct subscribers and those whose subscriptions are handled through agencies. It is easier and cheaper in the long run to bill and send other notices directly to all subscribers. Still another problem is the actual effectiveness of agents' claiming services. A recent article by Wernstedt showed that direct order claims were much more successful than those made through agents.[14] The critical change, however, is the discount, which was the margin of profit for agents in the past, and now, in its absence, is forcing them to charge ever-increasing fees to make ends meet.

SPECIAL PROBLEMS OF SCI-TECH LIBRARIES

The nature of science and technology libraries, their materials, services, and clients, create some unique factors in evaluating the use of subscription agents. First is that periodical and serial materials tend to be extremely important in the collections of sci-tech libraries. For example, in the small public library where this author worked for several years, there were fewer than 500 subscriptions, although they had more than 100,000 monographic titles and employed over twenty professional librarians. By contrast, one of the relatively small medical college libraries employing fewer than ten professional librarians maintains about 2,000 subscriptions. Estimates of the proportion of holdings in periodicals and serials in the libraries participating in this study ranged from 50% to 90%, while in the public library previously mentioned, they accounted for less than one percent. Second, research in science and technology requires access to the newest and most up-to-date material in a field, making frequently published periodicals a more immediate information source than monographs, which take much longer to produce. Other serials such as annuals, proceedings, etc., are very important, too. No matter how importance is measured—by budget allocation, number of titles, or percent of holdings—periodicals and serials measure very high. Third, the cost of science and technology periodicals is much higher than similar publications in other fields. In the *Library Journal* annual price index for 1982, the top six fields out of 24 listed in price averages were Chemistry and Physics (together), Medicine, Mathematics (including General Science, Botany and Geology), Engineering, Zoology, and Psychology, in that order. General interest periodicals were seventeenth on the list and other sci-tech-related fields rated fourteenth (Industrial Arts) and twentieth (Agriculture).[15] Another analysis of the cost of periodical titles contained in a series of subject-oriented indexes showed that, of fourteen fields where individual titles averaged over $100.00 a year, all were fields of science or technology.[16] The *Library Journal* analysis showed that the number of titles has increased, too, in all fields except Medicine, where they remained constant. The price differentials between sci-tech fields and social sciences or humanities is substantial, e.g., the average price of a chemistry/physics journal in 1982 was $177.94, a political science journal was $25.89, and a literature/language journal was $19.39.

The average cost of a law journal, a professional field, was $27.53.[17]

The importance of periodical and serial literature to the sci-tech researcher, the size of serial acquisitions compared to monographic acquisitions, and the cost of sci-tech serials are three factors which make decisions affecting this type of material vital to the ongoing development of science and technology libraries.

THE IMPACT OF NETWORKING

Sci-tech librarians whom this author interviewed while researching for this article discussed the importance to their operations of interlibrary loans as a source of periodical materials for their clients. Only one of the institutions said they neither lent nor received materials on interloan. Medical librarians in particular have created well-developed resource-sharing networks without which any one of them would have great difficulty supplying the broad range of costly materials needed. In addition, there is a growing number of special libraries joining bibliographic utilities or local/regional multitype networks offering enhanced resource-sharing as a high priority service. Some of the networks include sophisticated document delivery systems in their array of services.

Networking and sharing resources are some of the ways sci-tech libraries have been able to overcome financial problems resulting from a combination of events: availability of greater numbers of relevant titles in all subject fields; higher costs per title exacerbated by inflation in recent years; and limited budgets for materials during the last decade, decidedly a lean period for libraries. Some librarians reported their serials budget has been protected at the expense of monographic acquisitions, making serials more important than ever.

SURVEY ON CURRENT SERIALS ACQUISITIONS

A small sample of science and technology librarians was surveyed to determine whether or not their practices follow similar patterns. In all, eleven librarians from ten institutions were queried. The libraries serve two medical colleges, three corporations, one college, one professional group, and three divisions of a major university. The two smallest each had approximately 400 subscriptions. The others ranged, in ascending order, from 1,000 titles in the active order file to 35,000+ in the central unit of the university, and included libraries with 2,000, 3,000, 4,000, 5,000, 7,000 and 8,000 subscriptions in the middle ranges.

Agents were employed by all ten libraries and all but two used more than one. The main reason given for having more than one agent was that different agents were used to obtain foreign and domestic titles. Also, different agents were used to obtain periodicals, defined as journals having regular issues, and serials, defined as annuals, irregulars, and monographic series. One librarian used several agents to avoid putting all their eggs in one basket. All librarians purchased some titles directly from publishers as well.

When asked why they used subscription agents, the convenience they provide and the cost of doing it themselves were most frequently mentioned, with three librarians specifically saying it saved them at least one salary. Satisfaction with their agents' performance ranged from a qualified "reasonably so" to an enthusiastic "yes," with most (five out of eleven) giving some qualification to a generally positive reply. Some of these were: Agents need close monitoring; sometimes we have to bug them; hard to say because they do some things well and others not so well. One librarian who was satisfied with the current agent said there had been "clinkers" in the past. Several libraries have written contracts with their agents, but not all.

Asked to name the chief complaint against their agent(s), cost was the most frequent response (from five librarians), with delays in entering new subscriptions or responding to problems next (from four). Two librarians had no complaints, and one of these said they switched from a bad agent. Among the other negative comments received were that agents change their procedures without notifying clients; that fees seem to be set or changed arbitrarily; that agents don't pursue clients' claims vigorously enough; and that special supplements are often missed because agents don't know about them and don't alert librarians to order them, apparently because the announcements only appear in issues of the publications which agents and librarians do not read. In one library where two staff members—one from reference and one from technical services—answered the questions, the reference librarian complained of delays in receiving issues of titles on order, while her technical services counterpart said there were no complaints. Obviously, perceptions of speedy or slow service are subjective, depending on one's point of view.

Additional services clients wish their subscription agent would perform included the following:

1. Faster service in ironing out problems (two libraries named this);
2. Quarterly fiscal reports; a second said more reporting functions;
3. Stolen issue replacement service;
4. Better record keeping; and
5. Attend to irregularly-issued supplements.

Seven out of eight librarians were willing to pay a little more for these added services, but the eighth said they were paying enough as it is and the extra service should be without charge. Two other librarians did not want any extra services.

The final question in the survey asked librarians to rank the following five factors of serials acquisitions with or without a dealer in order of importance:

1. Cost, i.e., size of discount or service charge;
2. Amount of paperwork;
3. Time to obtain materials;
4. Gaps in subscription runs; and
5. Other services, i.e., cataloging, reporting, etc.

Six librarians ranked Time to obtain materials as their first concern, while only two ranked Cost first, two ranked Amount of paperwork first and one ranked Gaps in subscription runs first. Gaps in runs was the second-rank choice of seven librarians, while two others selected Cost as their second priority. One librarian ranked Time to obtain materials second behind Gaps in runs, and one ranked Paperwork second. For most of those surveyed, third and fourth choices were divided among Cost, Paperwork, Time, and Gaps. Everyone ranked Other services last. (See Table 1.)

One interesting observation in this small sample of libraries is the relatively minor importance attached to cost despite several years of the economic crunch caused by shrinking budgets, higher costs per title, and more journal titles. Two factors may have mitigated the adverse economic effects, i.e., protection of the serials budget at the

TABLE 1

IMPORTANCE OF FACTORS IN THE SERIALS ACQUISITION PROCESS

(n=11)

FACTOR	RANK 1	2	3	4	5
A. COST (Size of discount, or service charge)	2	2	4	3	0
B. PAPERWORK	2	1	4	3	0
C. TIME TO OBTAIN MATERIALS	6	1	2	1	0
D. GAPS IN SUBSCRIPTION RUNS	1	7	0	3	0
E. OTHER SERVICES (e.g., cataloging, reporting)	0	0	0	0	10

expense of monographic acquisitions and resource-sharing. Both were mentioned by the librarians surveyed.

Emphasis of science and technology librarians is on obtaining materials quickly and without missing issues. The convenience of using agents is related to cost, since staff time costs money. Several spoke about paying one bill instead of many as an advantage, although one person complained about problems with billing adjustments, an issue also raised by Paul. Dealing with billing changes and changes in the agents' fee structure are important problems raised by more than one respondent, but these did not generate as much heat as missing issues or delays in starting or stopping subscriptions. In this author's opinion, based on the investigation, costs of using subscription agents are perceived as being high—one said as much as $5.00 a title—but bearable so long as materials are received without problems or delays. Librarians seem ready to switch agents if they believe service can be improved. Only one of the librarians changed agents because of cost, and that institution was required to let bids every other year.

A final conclusion which can be drawn from this brief study is that science and technology librarians are not willing to do-it-themselves. Dispensing with agents' services still appears too formidable a task, even for libraries dealing with fewer than 5,000 titles. Paul's and Wernstedt's studies notwithstanding, subscription agents need not fear many librarians will opt to do without them.

SUMMARY

Reviewing the four questions posed at the beginning of this article, what answers may we formulate? First, who is correct about the value of subscription agents? Paul's case study and Wernstedt's massive study of claiming both suggest that money and time can be saved by doing without agents. In these large university library operations, there may be more flexibility in staffing and different kinds of costing (e.g., Paul says that the cost of issuing many checks is the problem of the accounting department, not the acquisitions librarian)[18] which make working without agents more appealing. For the majority of sci-tech librarians in this sample, and possibly, in the community at large, there are not enough staff members available to opt for direct subscription without new personnel. To be sure, the librarians say the amount and cost of paperwork agents save them is the best reason for using agents, but they prioritize speedy receipt of material ahead of cost and paperwork. This discrepancy needs clarification.

Second, those who question the use of agents base their opinions on their own research. There is a real need for more cost-benefit analyses of agent vs. no-agent serial acquisitions. Unfortunately, the "gut reaction" to direct subscription is "ALL THAT WORK!" rather than a more considered study of relative costs. If Paul is correct and it is more cost-effective to purchase serials directly from their publishers, it is hard not to imagine some librarians changing their *modus operandi.* It is not, however, universally true for everyone even if it is true for the University of Oregon.

Third, sci-tech librarians are using subscription agents, following Katz and Gellatly's rule of thumb (use an agent for 100+ titles) and they do not appear to be open to serious consideration of direct subscription. They seem to be aware of agents' shortcomings and appreciative of good service. The idea of switching to another agent seems more feasible than switching to direct subscription mode of acquisition.

Finally, in answer to the question of what criteria should be used to determine decisions, this author believes that the high cost of subscription services warrants careful and thorough study of alternatives, including the direct subscription approach. Decisions ought to be made on the basis of facts, not belief that things cannot be done in dramatically different ways. Once having performed such a study, librarians can rest assured their use of agents (or in its place, direct purchasing) is based on accurate analysis of their own situation, costs and benefits, and the real effect of the choice.

REFERENCES

1. Katz, Bill; Gellatly, Peter. *Guide to magazine and serial agents.* New York: Bowker; 1975: p. 3.
2. Paul, Huibert. Are subscription agents worth their keep? *The Serials Librarian.* 7 (1); 40; 1982 Fall.
3. Huff, William H. Serial subscription agencies. *Library Trends.* 24 (4); 690-692; 1976 April.
4. Ibid, p. 693.
5. *EBSCO subscription services.* Birmingham, Ala.: EBSCO: n.d.: p. 28. Emphasis added.
6. Ibid., p. 28.
7. Ibid., p. 3.
8. Ibid., p. 6.
9. Ibid.
10. *Turner subscription services.* New York: Turner Subscription Agency; 1982: p. 2.
11. Description of agents' services is derived from EBSCO and Turner marketing literature and sales catalogs.
12. Paul, op cit; p. 32.
13. Paul, op cit; p. 32-35.
14. Wernstedt, Irene J. The effectiveness of serials claiming. *Serials Review.* 8 (1); 45; 1982 Spring. In reporting on a massive study of the claiming problem done at the Pennsylvania State University Libraries, she says, "Direct order claims achieved the best success ratio . . . 82 percent for 1970-78 . . . our major domestic vendor achieved a 72 percent success ratio for 1970-78."
15. Brown, Norman D.; Phillips, Jane. Price indexes for 1982: U.S. periodicals and serial services. *Library Journal.* 107 (14); 1379; 1982 August.
16. Lowell, Gerald R. Periodical prices 1980-1982 update. *The Serials Librarian.* 7 (1); 79; 1982 Fall.
17. Brown, op cit; p. 1380-1381.
18. Paul, op cit; p. 40.

APPENDIX

INTERVIEW SCHEDULE FOR SCI/TECH LIBRARIANS

1. NAME & TITLE OF RESPONDENT:
2. NAME OF LIBRARY/TYPE OF LIBRARY—PARENT INSTITUTION:
3. RELATIVE SIZE OF LIBRARY BY # OF VOLUMES: # OF

CLIENTS SERVED: # OF CIRCULATIONS OR TRANSACTIONS: OR # OF STAFF:

4. IMPORTANCE OF PERIODICALS IN COLLECTION BY % OF TOTAL HOLDINGS AND/OR # OF TITLES HELD:

5. IS THIS FIGURE (FROM QUESTION 4) HIGHER OR LOWER THAN IT HAS BEEN IN PREVIOUS YEARS? SAME?

6. IS USE OF THE PERIODICAL COLLECTION HEAVIER OR LIGHTER THAN IN PREVIOUS YEARS? SAME?

7. DO YOU USE A SUBSCRIPTION AGENT? MORE THAN ONE?

8. WHY? (IF NOT, GO TO QUESTION 12)

9. ARE YOU SATISFIED THAT THE AGENT IS FULFILLING YOUR NEEDS/EXPECTATIONS/CONTRACT?

10. WHAT ADDITIONAL SERVICES DO YOU WISH THE AGENT WOULD PERFORM? WOULD YOU PAY MORE FOR THESE SERVICES?

11. WHAT IS YOUR CHIEF COMPLAINT ABOUT YOUR SUBSCRIPTION AGENT(S)?

12. IF YOU DO NOT USE AN AGENT, WHAT IS YOUR CHIEF COMPLAINT ABOUT YOUR CURRENT MODE OF OPERATIONS?

13. RANK THE FOLLOWING ATTRIBUTES ACCORDING TO THEIR IMPORTANCE TO YOU IN EVALUATING YOUR PERIODICAL OPERATION:
    — SIZE OF DISCOUNT/SERVICE CHARGES.
    — AMOUNT OF PAPERWORK.
    — TIME TO OBTAIN MATERIALS.
    — GAPS IN SUBSCRIPTIONS' RUNS.
    — OTHER SERVICES SUCH AS CATALOGING, ETC.
    — OTHER? (IF NONE OF THE ABOVE ARE 1ST RANK.)

Selection and Evaluation of Chemistry Periodicals

Barbara A. Rice

ABSTRACT. The difficulties of selecting or evaluating a chemistry periodicals collection are described. The author compares 5 sets of chemistry titles selected by 5 techniques; a use study, standard lists (CASSI and JCR), faculty recommendation, and an on-line collection development service. The results are analyzed and discussed in terms of periodicals collection development practices.

An evaluation of a library's collection is, in effect, an evaluation of its selection methods, as George Bonn points out in "Evaluation of the Collection."[1] A librarian decides what titles should be added to an existing collection on an individual basis, and then evaluates the composite decisions in a collection evaluation. The techniques used for both selection and evaluation are the same, and will be viewed as opposite faces of the same coin by this author.

Nowhere are the librarian's selection decisions more difficult than in the field of chemistry, where periodicals abound, prices are high, the periodicals are extremely important to users, and there is plenty of advice in the literature about preferred selection methods.

Periodicals are extremely important to chemists. Heinzkill[2] reports that 93.6% of chemists' citations are to journals, as compared to 91.8% by physicists, 80.8% by zoologists, 76.8% by math-

---

Barbara A. Rice is Principal Librarian, Reference Services, New York State Library, Albany, NY 12230. This paper is based on information gathered when Ms. Rice was science bibliographer at the State University of New York at Albany, University Library. Ms. Rice holds an MLS from University of California at Berkeley and a BS (Chemistry) from the University of Massachusetts. Her work experience includes service in special libraries, an academic library, and most recently in the New York State Library where she is responsible for reference and collection development activities.

© 1983 by The Haworth Press, Inc. All rights reserved.

ematicians, 41.9% by sociologists, and 23.3% by historians. A greater proportion of a science library's budget is devoted to serials than to monographs, reflecting this importance. Bourne and Gregor[3] report that 96%, 93% and 86% of the total acquisition budget at one major university was spent for chemistry, biology and public health serials respectively in 1973/74. Such figures usually lead library directors to exert pressure to reduce the proportion of the budget spent on science serials. The failure of library budgets to keep pace with inflationary increases in subscription costs increases this pressure on the science periodicals, especially those in chemistry and physics.

The 1982 price indexes for periodicals[4] again showed chemistry and physics titles as the most expensive in the 24 subject categories reported. The average 1982 subscription price for all categories was $44.80, but the average 1982 subscription price for chemistry and physics periodicals was $177.94. Chemistry and physics titles have been the most expensive for years, although the percentage increase in cost per year has not been as high as for some other fields, such as zoology and medicine.

In addition to being important and expensive, chemistry titles are plentiful. In 1976 *Chemical Abstracts* routinely scanned 16,062 titles for chemical information, and the number is rising.[5] Given these factors the bibliographers, chemistry librarians, or special librarians have a difficult task in selecting those titles which they project will be in greatest demand by the chemists they serve. It is unlikely that any of these librarians have sufficient budgets to purchase all titles needed, but they are constantly evaluating what titles will be purchased in a given year or period of years.

Just as there is no shortage of expensive titles from which to choose, there is no shortage of recommended techniques or models which can be used to decide on individual titles to add, or which titles to retain. In an excellent article Singleton[6] summarizes the diversity of methods available, citing some 60 titles relating to selection. He then compares these methods for the literature of physics. The main methods of ranking titles (the most highly ranked presumably being the best selections) are citation analyses, use or user judgment, and size or productivity ratings. Singleton found on the whole little correlation between lists generated by the different methods. He suggested that a similar study comparing these techniques for a particular user group and set of journal holdings might be useful.

METHODOLOGY FOR COMPARISON OF FIVE TECHNIQUES FOR SELECTING CHEMISTRY JOURNALS

The author had the opportunity to evaluate the chemistry collection of a medium-sized university library over a period of several years. All science periodicals were housed in one collection and not separated in branch libraries. The major interests of the chemistry department were biochemistry, organic and physical chemistry and environmental chemistry. The study began when the bibliographers were given responsibility for reviewing the periodicals collection for cancellation, storage and discard decisions. A major handicap to the decision-making process was the fact that periodicals did not circulate, nor was there any other use information available. The author designed and conducted a use study of the 2,300 science titles held by the library. This was reported in detail in the *Serials Librarian*.[7] Also reported was a comparison of the lists of most heavily used titles with those ranked in *Journal Citation Reports*.[8] Little correlation was found, a situation similar to that reported by Scales[9] and the work already mentioned by Singleton.[6] Garfield in the introduction to *Journal Citation Reports*[8] advised that caution is advisable in comparing journals from different disciplines.

This paper concentrates on chemistry journals only, and compares the results obtained in the use study with rankings on a standard list (CASSI), and same titles in JCR, a set of faculty recommendations and titles cited in an on-line collection development service. The primary difficulty in these comparisons is to define a chemistry periodical. Since the collection studied was classified in Library of Congress classification scheme, this could have been used. However, based on experience, this would have excluded important chemistry titles. The author decided to use *Chemical Abstracts,* "List of 1000 Journals Most Frequently Cited in *Chemical Abstracts*"[10] as the base list for definition of a chemistry title. All of the library's titles classified in QD are on the list, as are a great number classified in QC, QH, QP and TP also. Chemical Abstracts Service scans periodicals for reports of new chemical information to be announced and abstracted by the service, and the 1,000 most frequently cited were, for the purposes of this paper, considered to be chemistry journals. Table 1 lists the 100 top ranked titles from that list, and beside each title gives the overall rank in the periodical's use study and also the 1975 *Journal Citation Reports* rank. It must be pointed out that relative positions on the CASSI and

Table 1

Periodicals Study Overall Rankings

Journal Name	Ranking		
	CASSI	USE	JCR
Biochim. Biophy. Acta	1	8	5
J. Amer. Chem. Soc.	2	6	1
J. Chem. Phy.	3	67	3
Dokl. Akad. Nauk. SSR	4	86	56
J. Org. Chem.	5	57	22
Tetrahedron Lett.	6	72	31
J. Chem. Soc., Chem. Comm.	7	86	39
Zhurnal Fiz Khim.	8	85	214
J. Biol. Chem.	9	7	2
Phys. Rev. B.	10	74	32
Bull. Chem. Soc. Jap.	11	85	78
Biochem. Biophys. Res. Comm.	12	27	16
Izv. Akad. Nauk SSR Ser. Khim.	13	87	283
Chem. Phys. Lett.	14	71	75
C. R. Acad. Sci. Ser. C.	15	87	280
Zh. Obshch. Khim.	16	87	149
Fiz. Tverd. Tela (Leningrad)	17	16	341
C. R. Acad. Sci. Ser. D.	18	84	212
Phys. Rev. Lett.	19	54	11
Zh. Neorg. Khim.	20	84	218
Nucl. Phys. A.	91	65	47
Phys. Lett. A.	22	84	111
Inorg. Chem.	23	82	40
Zh. Prikl. Khim. (Leningrad)	24	not used	521
Biochem. J.	25	32	10
Proc. Nat. Acad. Sci. (U.S.A.)	26	9	8
Zh. Org. Khim.	27	87	364
J. Appl. Phys.	28	62	24
J. Phys. Chem.	29	77	29
FEBS Lett.	30	57	64
Proc. Soc. Exp. Biol. Med.	31	77	28
Biochemistry	32	17	12
Bull. Soc. Chim. Fr.	33	86	77

Table 1 - Continued
Periodicals Study Overall Rankings

Journal Name	Ranking		
	CASSI	USE	JCR
J. Organomet. Chem.	34	66	76
Phys. Lett. B.	35	80	57
Phytochemistry	36	82	164
Experientia	37	78	99
Phys. Rev. D.	38	84	62
Phys. Status Solidi A.	39	84	363
J. Chromat.	40	60	80
Nature (London) New Biol.	41	-	-
Solid State Commun.	42	84	113
Anal. Chem.	43	45	27
J. Inorg. Nucl. Chem.	44	82	108
J. Chem. Soc., Perkin Trans. 1	45	83	-
Can. J. Chem.	46	74	68
Acta. Chem. Scand.	47	77	78
Phys. Status Solidi. B.	48	81	270
J. Chem. Soc., Dalton Trans.	49	87	219
Eur. J. Biochem.	50	39	41
J. Bacteriology	51	54	31
J. Chem. Soc., Perkin Trans. 2	52	87	-
Izv. Akad. Nauk. SSSR, Neorg. Mater.	53	not in lib	885
Nucl. Instrum. Meth.	54	77	144
Izv. Vyssh. Ucheb. Zaved., Khim. Khim. Tekhnol.	55	not in lib	-
J. Phys. Soc. Jap.	56	79	82
Phys. Rev. C.	57	not used	122
Fiz. Tekh. Poluprov.	58	68	518
Science	59	1	7
Acta. Crystallog., Sect. B.	60	80	153
Endocrinology	61	84	33
Arch. Biochem. Biophys.	62	28	36
Zavod. Lab.	63	not in lib	491
Elektrokhimiya	64	not in lib	-
Khim. Geterotsikl. Soedin.	65	not used	621

Table 1 - Continued

Periodicals Study Overall Rankings

Journal Name	Ranking		
	CASSI	USE	JCR
J. Pharm. Sci.	66	72	128
Chem. Pharm. Bull.	67	84	225
Collect. Czech. Chem. Commun.	68	not in lib.	182
Nippon Kagaku Kaishi	69	not used	1,082
Nucl. Phys. B.	70	85	102
J. Mol. Biol.	71	17	15
J. Chem. Educ.	72	55	437
Appl. Phys. Lett.	73	81	73
Tetrahedron	74	80	66
Nature	75	3	4
Izv. Akad. Nauk. SSSR, Ser. Fiz.	76	not in lib.	431
Zh. Prikl. Spektrosk.	77	86	-
Zh. Anal. Khim.	78	86	324
Arzneim - Forsch.	79	not in lib.	217
Opt. Spektrosk.	80	not in lib.	337
Met. Trans.	81	not in lib.	-
Anal. Biochem.	82	56	55
Indian J. Chem.	83	86	519
J. Immunol.	84	71	34
Agr. Biol. Chem.	85	not in lib.	312
Phys. Rev. A.	86	74	58
J. Electrochem. Soc.	87	75	119
Chem. Ber.	88	85	44
Fiz. Metal. Metalloved.	89	87	445
Vysokomol. Soedin., Ser. A.	90	87	258
Clin. Chim. Acta	91	80	114
J. Med. Chem.	92	84	212
Izv. Vyssh. Ucheb. Zaved., Fiz.	93	not in lib.	993
J. Phys. C.	94	83	176
Zh. Eksp. Teor. Fiz.	95	87	84
J. Phys. (Paris) Colloq.	96	not in lib.	504
C. R. Acad. Sci., Ser. B.	97	-	475
C. R. Soc. Biol.	98	not in lib.	288
Biochem. Pharmacol.	99	not in lib.	94
J. Cryst. Growth	100	86	427

JCR lists change each year, although the same journals persist on the lists over many years. The numbers on these lists must be viewed as positions relative to each other. The numbers should *NOT* be considered as having any absolute value. This table is included so that the reader can see the most productive chemistry journals as listed in CASSI and compare the ranks obtained in a use study and a ranking prepared by citation analysis of science periodicals, JCR.

In preparing the analysis for chemistry journals, the author listed titles in the rank order in which they appeared in the use study, rather than alphabetically. She believed Line's statement that "no measure of journal use other than one derived from a local-use study is of any significant, practical value to libraries,"[11] and wished to compare the results of the other techniques to the use study. The most used chemistry titles in the previously mentioned State University of New York at Albany (SUNYA) study are listed in rank order in Table 2. A rank of 32 represents a total of 4 users over a two-semester period, and a rank of 33 represents three uses. After that there were large numbers of titles showing one or two uses which are not reported in this paper. Only the 111 most used titles are listed in rank order in the first column of Table 2. Then the CASSI rank is given in the second column. Examination of the two columns show that there is little similarity between relative rank positions on the two lists.

In order to derive a JCR ranking for chemistry titles, a card was made for each of the 111 titles, and the JCR rank recorded on the card. The cards were then placed in order from "most cited" and renumbered from 1 to 111 giving their relative positions in the overall list. So that the reader will have some idea of the actual JCR ranks, that number is given for every 10th ranked item on the list. Again the reader must remember that the use numbers and the JCR numbers represent relative positions, relative numbers of uses or times cited.

The author was able to investigate how faculty evaluations of importance compare to use for one segment of the user population, organic chemists. The faculty had asked that a list of "important" periodical titles be added to a guide to the library's holdings in organic chemistry that the author had compiled. Rather than selecting the titles herself the author asked the faculty to select the most important titles from the CASSI "1000 Most Frequently Cited List." They selected 42 titles. These are marked with an "X" in the fourth column of Table 2 labeled Fac. Select. They also selected 13 titles

Table 2

Comparative Rankings

Journal Name	SUNYA Rank	CASSI	Rel. JCR	Fac. Selec.	BRS
Science	1	59	6	X	9
Nature	2	41	4		9
J. American Chemical Society	3	2	1	X	3
J. Biological Chemistry	4	9	2	X	6
Biochim. Biophys. Acta	5	1	5		8
Proc. National Acad. Sci.	6	26	7	X	6
Biochemistry	7	32	12		5
Archives of Biochem. Biophys.	8	62	15		
Analytical Chemistry	9	43	11	X	10
Annal. N. Y. Acad. Sci.	10	–	16		
Physical Review Letters	11	19	8		9
J. Chem. Educ.	12	72	86	X	
J. Organic Chemistry	13	5	9	X	5
Industrial and Engineering Chem.	14	770	66		
J. Chromatography	15	40	31		
J. Applied Physics	16	29	10 (24)		8
Chemical and Engineering News	17	878	106		
Nuclear Physics. A.	18	21	20 (47)		
J. Organometallic Chem.	19	34	28	X	12
J. Chemical Physics	20	3	3	X	1
Chem. Phys. Letters	21	14	27		2
Chemical Week	21				
Tetrahedron Letters	22	6	13	X	11
Canadian J. Chem.	23	46	23	X	11
Physical Review A	23	86	14		5
Physical Review B. Solid State	23	10			
Acta Chemica Scandinavica	24	47	25	X	
Acta Crystallographica	24	60	32		12
J. Electrochemical Society	24	87	43	X	
Chemical Engineering	25	721	102		
Chemistry and Industry	25	380	68	X	12

Table 2 - Continued

Comparative Rankings

Journal Name	SUNYA Rank	CASSI	Rel. JCR	Fac. Selec.	BRS
Soviet Physics Solid State	25	17	76		
J. Chromatographic Science	25	732	87		
Proceedings Royal Society of London	25	853	19		
Angewandte Chemie	26	126	40 (110)	X	
J. Physical Chemistry	26	29	12	X	
Nuclear Instruments and Methods	26	54	46		
J. Physics B. At. Mol. Phys.	26	70	286		4
Applied Optics	27	125	50 (152)		
Experientia	27	37	35	X	12
J. Catalysis	27	156	69		
J. Assoc. of Official Anal. Chemists	28	278	82		
Biopolymers	28	457	63		5
Chemical Engineering Science	28	134	74		
Physics Letters B	28	35	21		
Tetrahedron	28	74	24	X	
Applied Physics Letters	29	73	26		
Coordination Chemistry Reviews	29		97		
Molecular Physics	29	166	51		
Phys. Stat. Solidi. B. Basic Research	29	48	75		
Canadian J. Physics	30	378	48		12
High Temperature	30	661	109		
Inorganic Chemistry	30	23	17	X	
J. Inorganic and Nuclear Chem.	30	44	39		8
J. Physics and Chemistry of Solids	30	290	38		
Physica	30	A 668 B+C 325	60 (219)		
Accounts of Chem. Research	31	971	72		
Analyst	31	287	77		
Applied Physics	31	307			
J. Chem. Soc. London. Perkin Trans. 1	31	45	56	X	12

Table 2 - Continued

Comparative Rankings

Journal Name	SUNYA Rank	CASSI	Rel. JCR	Fac. Selec.	BRS
Electrochimica Acta	31	204	88		
Fortschritte der Chemischen Forschung	31				
Justus Liebigs' Ann. der Chemie	31	293	36	X	12
Helvetica Chimica Acta	31	217	33	X	
J. Physics C	31	3			
J. Polymer Science	31				9
Photochemistry and Photobiology	31	275	84		
Analytica Chimica Acta	32	96	54		
Acad. des Sciences Comptes Rendus. Ser. D. Sci. Naturelles	32	18	57		
J. Chem. Documentation	32		107		
J. Electroanalytical Chem. and Interfacial Electrochem.	32	130	64		12
J. Heterocyclic Chem.	32	108	93		
J. Medicinal Chemistry	32	92	55	X	10
J. Molecular Spectroscopy	32	196	62		10
Nuovo Cimento	32	448	44		
Philosophical Magazine	32	470			12
Phys. Stat. Solidi A. Applied Research	32	39	79		
Phys. Rev. D. Particles and Fields	32	38	22		
Physics, Letters A	32	22	41		12
Pure and Applied Chemistry	32	283	89		12
Organomettalic Compounds	32				
Russian J. Inorganic Chem.	32	20	59	X	
Solid State Communications	32	42	42		
Theoretica Chimica Acta	32	580	73		
Zeitschrift fur Kristallographie, Kristallgeom., Kristallphysik	32	343	94		
Zeitschrift fur Physik	33	281	34		
Biochimie	33	510	95		
Catalysis Reviews-Science and Engineering	33		108		

Table 2 - Continued

Comparative Rankings

Journal Name	SUNYA Rank	CASSI	Rel. JCR	Fac. Selec.	BRS
Chemical Technology	33	614	104		
Chemische Berichte	33	88	18	X	12
Chemistry	33				
Chemical Reviews	33		53		
Fresenius Zeitschrift fur Anal. Chem.	33	238	85		8
Int. J. Environmental Anal. Chem.	33				12
Int. J. Mass Spectrometry and Ion Physics	33	423			12
J. Chem. Information and Computer Sciences	33				
J. Colloid and Interface Science	33	110	67		
J. Macromol. Sci. Part C. Reviews	33	323	111		
J. Polymer Sci. Polymer Physics Ed.	33	328	81		9
J. Quantitative Spectroscopy and Radiative Transfer	33	594	91		
J. Radioanalytical Chem.	33	219	103		
J. Optical Society of America	33	955	37		
Molecular Crystals and Liquid Crystals	33	406	98		10
Bull. Chem. Society of Japan	33	11	30	X	11
Polymer J.	33	691	101		12
Radiation Effects	33	228	96		
Radiochemical and Radioanalytical Letters	33	354	105		12
Review of Scientific Instruments	33	251	45		12
Russian J. Physical Chem.	33	8	58		8
Talanta	33	256	78		10
Zeitschrift fur Anorganische und Allgemeine Chemie	33	150	47	X	

Table 2 - Continued

Comparative Rankings

Journal Name	SUNYA Rank	CASSI	Rel. JCR	Fac. Selec.	BRS
Added Faculty Selections					
J. Chemical Society. Chem. Comm.	34	7	18	X	
Izv. Akad. Nauk. SSSR. Ser. Khim	35	13	71	X	
Acad. des. Sciences. Comptes Rendus. Ser. C.	35	15	70	X	12
Russian J. General Chemistry	35	16	49	X	10
Russian J. Organic Chemistry	35	27	80	X	11
J. Chem. Soc. Dalton Trans.	35	49	65	X	10
J. Chem. Soc. Perkin Trans. 2	35	52	not sep.	X	not sep.
Indian J. Chemistry	34	83	90	X	
Australian J. Chemistry	34	164	61	X	12
Bull. Soc. Chim. de France	34	434	29	X	
J. Magnetic Resonance	35	213	92	X	
J. Chem. Soc. Faraday Trans. 1	35	211	83	X	12
Synthesis	35	157	100 716	X	12
Added BRS Highly Ranked					
J. Electron Spectros. and Related Phenomena		634			5
Chemical Physics	not in lib.	153			5
European Polymer Journal	34	262	99		5
Doklady Akad. Nauk. SSSR	34	4	21		6
Inorganica Chimica Acta	34	67	88		6
Opt. Spektrosk.	not in lib.	80	76		6
Studies in Biophysics		506	105		6
Vyosokomol Soedin Ser. A	34	90	65		7
Bioinorganic Chem.	not in lib.		110		8
Agricult. Biol. Chem.	not in lib.	85	74		9
Macromolecules	35	154	81		9

which did not appear in the most heavily used group. These journals are found near the end of Table 2 in the section titled "Added Faculty Selections." All of the titles selected by the faculty as "important had shown at least one use in the study. Overall for this specific subset of users, organic chemists, there is good agreement between what the faculty consider important and what is in actuality used.

Another method of identifying important titles, and especially new ones, derives from the ease of compiling lists of journals cited during on-line searches. It is well known that initiation of on-line search services in a library frequently means an increase in the number of interlibrary loan requests, as users are alerted to titles of interest in journals not held by the library. The SUNYA University Library had subscribed to BRS' (Bibliographic Retrieval Service) Collection Development Service, and in a one-year period, 832 journals were cited in 31 *Chemical Abstracts* searches. Ranks for the titles which appeared in the use study are given in the last column in Table 2. The range of ranks is small, as the distribution looked like this.

Rank	Number of Titles	Times Cited
1	1	33
2	1	13
3	1	11
4	1	9
5	8	8
6	6	7
7	3	6
8	8	5
9	18	4
10	29	3
11	73	2
12	683	1

Many highly ranked titles on the BRS list were not heavily used or were not in the library's collection. These are given at the end of Table 2, in the section titled "Added BRS Highly Ranked."

IMPLICATIONS FOR COLLECTION DEVELOPMENT

The American Library Association's *Guidelines for Collection Development* point out that library collections are established for a definite purpose, for research or teaching, and that a given collection is serving this purpose.

Standard lists, such as CASSI, are often used in collection evaluations and have a number of advantages relating to ease of application, but a distinct disadvantage in that any "standard list" may not be as representative of the library's subjects or purposes as its holdings are."[13] This is well illustrated by a cursory exmaination of the first two columns in Table 2. If the CASSI list had been used for selection or evaluation, *Industrial and Engineering Chemistry, Chemical and Engineering News, Chemical Engineering, Chemistry and Industry, Journal of Chromatographic Science, Proceedings of the Royal Society of London,* and *Angewandte Chemie* would not have been among the first 100 titles selected. Yet they were among the top 25 ranked by use. Indeed the library had only 53% of the titles on the "1000 Most Frequently Cited List."

There is no one list which can match the unique purposes of a given collection. Several of the titles just mentioned fulfill a current awareness or teaching function, although they do not report primarily new chemical information. Others of these titles represent the specialized interests of the community served, such as the *Journal of Chromatographic Science, Journal of Catalysis, Biopolymers* and *Molecular Physics.*

Citation lists, such as *Journal Citation Reports* are often used as evaluation tools because of their ready availability and because they, too, represent a type of use, that of being cited in a research paper. Citation and in-house use represent different things, as can be seen by examination of Table 2. In-house studies show significant use of current awareness journals which do not rank high in the CASSI list (which ranks based on amount of new chemical information reported) or the JCR list (which ranks based on citation frequency in research journals). However, given the difference in what is being measured, relative positions in columns 1 (use) and 3 (JCR rank) are quite similar. This would support Garfield's assertions that the most cited journals would tend to be most used if journals in the same discipline are compared. (He does, however, point out that there are distinct differences amongst the subfields of chemistry in terms of which journals yield the greatest number of citations. See Garfield[14] for a comparison of titles cited by *Journal of the American Chemical Society* and *Biochemistry*). With few exceptions a person using JCR as a selection/evaluation tool would have arrived at many of the same titles as those found in the user survey for this particular group of chemists and students.

Librarians in an academic or special library are usually assisted by their users in the selection and evaluation process. As this study shows, organic chemists' selections correlated well with use. Faculty advice then, although sometimes distrusted by librarians, should suggest titles which will probably be used. Their assistance in collection evaluation should also be encouraged. In some cases the librarian has the final say on purchase of recommended titles; in other cases the responsibility rests with the faculty or research staff served. If the librarian has final responsibility, he/she often attempts to evaluate a recommended title in some way, i.e., is its content accessible through a standard abstracting/indexing service (usually "yes in the case of chemistry), and is it apt to show use by more than one user? Evaluating the latter is difficult without adding the title and seeing who uses it, or by analyzing interlibrary loan requests to see if others have needed it, but perhaps not requested it. Sometimes, too, the librarian looks at the ranking in *Journal Citation Reports*. If the recommended title shows low rank compared to other titles already in the collections, it may be a marginal candidate. None of these techniques, however, helps with a newly published title.

Newly published titles is an area in which the on-line services can be valuable. Citations show up here before they reach heavily cited lists or before the titles have been suggested by librarian or faculty members for addition to the collection. The section of Table 2 titled "Added BRS Highly Ranked" shows that the *Journal of Electron Spectroscopy and Related Phenomena* and *Bioinorganic Chemistry* were highly ranked in the BRS Collection Development Service. The *Journal of Electron Spectroscopy and Related Phenomena* was held by the library at the time of the study, but there were, as yet, no bound volumes and hence no recorded use. *Bioinorganic Chemistry* was not in the library, but was later requested by a faculty member for addition to the collection. *Chemical Physics* was not in the library, but a subscription was later initiated. Some of the titles would be good candidates for purchase based on the BRS listing and relatively high JCR ranking.

With the exception of the titles for which bound volumes were not yet available each title on the BRS list had shown one or more uses. The collection development service seems to be a good way of identifying new titles of potential research value. They may not end up being highly used, but are likely to be requested by faculty doing research in specialized areas.

CONCLUSIONS

The discussion in this paper and the reader's analysis of Table 2 should reveal that there is no one method of selection which can identify all titles which will serve all purposes of a chemistry or other science collection. It is also unlikely that any evaluation method, such as determining the proportion of titles held on a standard list, will give a valid measure of the quality of the collection.

A use study is very time consuming and will tell you only what is used, not what may be needed. A citation study will tell you what is likely to be used for research, but not what current awareness or review titles supporting instruction are needed. Faculty recommendations are good indicators of what may be used, but there are usually more recommended titles than the budget can support. The situation with respect to online databases is less clear from this study, primarily because of the small sample of information available. As the collection development service continues, results between years should be compared and titles cumulated.

Any selection decision or collection evaluation should be recognized as a subjective judgment, no matter what quantitative or comparative techniques are used. The author hopes that the information presented here will provide others who have not had an opportunity to analyze their own collections with an appreciation of the complexity of the selection and evaluation processes and the knowledge that different techniques produce different results.

REFERENCES

1. Bonn, George S. Evaluation of the collection. *Library Trends.* 22(3):265-304; 1974 January.

2. Heinzkill, Richard. Characteristics of references in selected scholarly English literary journals. *Library Quarterly.* 50(3):352-365; 1980 July.

3. Bourne, Charles P.; Gregor, Dorothy. Planning serials cancellations and cooperative collection development in the health sciences: methodology and background information. *Bulletin of the Medical Library Association.* 63(4):366-377; 1975 October.

4. Brown, Norman B.; Phillips, Jane. Price indexes for 1982, U. S. periodicals and serial services. *Library Journal.* 107(14):1379-1382; 1982 August.

5. Dayton, David L. et al. CASSI:File for document access. *Special Libraries.* 69(9): 337-347; 1978 September.

6. Singleton, Alan. Journal ranking and selection: a review in physics. *Journal of Documentation.* 32(4);258-289; 1976 December.

7. Rice, Barbara A. Science periodicals use study. *Serials Librarian.* 4(1):35-47; 1979 Fall.

8. *Journal Citation Reports. Science Citation Index.* Philadelphia: Institute for Scientific Information; 1975-. Annual.

9. Scales, Pauline A. Citation analyses as indicators of the use of serials: a comparison of ranked title lists produced by citation counting and from use data. *Journal of Documentation.* 32(1):17-25; 1976 March.

10. List of 1,000 journals most frequently cited in Chemical Abstracts: *Chemical Abstracts Service Source Index.* Columbus, Ohio: American Chemical Society; 1980-. Annual.

11. Line, Maurice B. Rank lists based on citations and library uses as indicators of journal usage in individual libraries. *Collection Management.* 2(4):313-315; 1978 Winter.

12. Perkins, David L. ed. *Guidelines for collection development.* Chicago: American Library Association; 1979.

13. Ibid. p. 14.

14. Garfield, Eugene. Citation indexing. New York: Wiley; 1979. 163-165.

Selecting Multispecialty Mathematics Research Journals via Their Underlying Subject Emphases

Tony Stankus
Virgil Diodato

Mathematicians are like Frenchmen: whatever you say to them they translate into their own language and forthwith it is something completely different.

Goethe, *Maximen und Reflexionen*[1]

ABSTRACT. The problems of selecting mathematics research journals are reviewed, with particular emphasis on the best matching of multispecialty mathematics journals with given mathematical specialties. A simple method involving *Mathematical Reviews* classification numbers identified the specialties of 21,332 papers published between 1972 and 1979 in 30 multispecialty mathematics journals. The journals' underlying subject strengths are reported and compared. This reveals strong subject biases in several journals as well as a general pattern of subject polarization. The results are discussed in light of the current academic politics of Pure Mathematics versus Applied Mathematics.

INTRODUCTION

A librarian building a journal collection for pure and applied mathematicians often sees publishing patterns not usually encountered in other sci-tech literatures. Few sci-tech selection guide-

---

Mr. Stankus is Science Librarian, Science Library, College of the Holy Cross, Worcester, MA 01610. He holds the MLS from the University of Rhode Island at Kingston. Dr. Diodato holds the PhD in Library and Information Science from the University of Illinois at Urbana-Champaign. He is currently Assistant Professor at the School of Library and Information Science, University of Wisconsin-Milwaukee, P.O. Box 413, Milwaukee, WI 53201.

lines seem to apply to mathematics. The typical sci-tech literature in any given country and field is characterized by one or two general journals (such as the *Journal of the American Chemical Society*) and a large family of clearly designated subspecialty journals (such as *Biochemistry, Inorganic Chemistry,* and *Macromolecules*). In mathematics the United States alone has over a dozen essentially general journals, while families of mathematics journals seem easier to characterize by article length than by subspecialty. The publishing of most other sci-tech journal literature has become monopolized by the major national professional societies and well-known commercial houses. However, in mathematics these sources share roughly equal status with individual university presses (Illinois, Duke, Oxford); regional associations (Rocky Mountain Mathematics Consortium, London Mathematical Society, the sixteen institutions that together support the *Pacific Journal of Mathematics*); and less familiar commercial houses (Sithoff, Birkhauser, DeGruyter). While most other types of American scientists consistently read and publish within only American journals or those foreign titles characterized by English-language articles and American formats and schedules, American mathematicians are exceptionally cosmopolitan in their reading and choice of publishing outlets.[2-4] American mathematics journals feature French-language and German-language papers, with Italian occasionally seen. Even Latin is found in at least one prominent journal, the *Archive for Rational Mechanics and Analysis*.

While the journals of many of the other (generally larger) sci-tech disciplines annually have been ranked convincingly by *Journal Citation Reports*[5] in gross citations or impact factors—a process that promotes a consensus on journal selection between librarian and clientele—the results involving mathematics journals are usually not as clear. Factors in mathematics such as the higher frequency of citations to monographs, the lower rate of citations per paper, and the relatively small volume of papers in the field may be responsible.[6,7] There is uncertainty in the interpretation of the more complicated citing and cited relationships as well. In many other sci-tech disciplines, specialty journals that significantly cite more general journals in the same discipline are reassuringly cited in return, confirming a link in the mind of the collection developer. In mathematics this "love" often seems unrequited. For example, compare the citations made by the *Journal of Differential Equations* with those made by the *Transactions of the American Mathematical Society*, or those of the *Journal of Combinatorial Theory* with those of the *Proceedings* of the same society.

One strategy in the selection of mathematics journals would be to reverse the usual sci-tech selection procedure and first select the specialty journals that match the clientele before selecting any general journals. But this only delays the inevitable quandary about which of the more general journals to select. Guides such as Fedunok,[8] while being noteworthy for denoting the fields stressed in some journals, still tend to emphasize whether or not given titles are too technical for some collections. Contemporary guides to the general field or sci-tech literature (Malinowsky, Chen, Subramanyam)[9,10,11] and those specifically devoted to Mathematics (Pemberton, Dorling, Dick)[12,13,14] stress reference works and monographs. Attempts to sort journals by direct inspection of their content is likely to be frustrating for the librarian in light of mathematics' incredible terminology. Our study demonstrates a method, accessible to the librarian, of bypassing the terminology and of identifying the underlying subject strengths, where they exist, of mathematics research journals that each cover several specialties. We have labelled such journals as multispecialty journals.

METHODS

The journals involved in this study were chosen because they together covered various areas of mathematics, they were perceived as important by librarians and faculty at the authors' institutions, and they represented both American and non-American titles. As a practical matter, their number was limited to 30, although many other journals did meet our criteria. The first author of each paper appearing in these journals between 1972 and 1979 was searched in the 1972 through 1981 issues of *Mathematical Reviews (MR)*. Data gathered from *MR* were the first two digits of the primary subject classification code assigned to each paper. (A recent brief explanation of the classification system used by *MR* is in Kusma.[15] Major headings of the system are displayed on the front cover of most *MR* issues.) These codes were grouped into ten specialty categories modified from earlier work by Diodato.[16] And so, each paper was easily placed in one of the following specialty fields: mathematical foundations (including logic, set theory, combinatorics, universal algebra), algebra and group theory, algebraic geometry, complex and harmonic analysis, ordinary differential equations, partial differential equations, real and abstract analysis, differential geometry, topology, applied mathematics (including statistics, probability, numerical analysis). The process of categorization was straightforward and certainly required no special insight into mathematical terminology. The list of journals, the specialty field categories and corresponding *MR* classification codes, and the raw data for each journal are in the Appendices.

RESULTS

One result is clear from even a cursory glance at Tables 1-4. There is indeed substantial variation in subject emphasis among multispecialty mathematics research journals. In almost every specialty category there are some journals that devote much of their content to that field while others provide almost nothing. The selection of the appropriate multispecialty journal for matching with a clientel's specialties should not be a matter of random choice. Yet, if selection in these instances should not be random, should it be a matter for individual journal analysis every time a journal subscription is considered? While we later will argue for the ease and merit of making such individual determinations, the reader should be aware that there are some general characteristics of journals that ought to allow the librarian to make preliminary decisions for groups of journals.

A comparison of the results in Tables 1 and 2 suggests that there is an inverse relationship of specialty strengths for at least two sets of specialty fields. One set is algebra and group theory, algebraic geometry, and topology. The other is ordinary differential equations, partial differential equations, and applied mathematics. Comparisons here are based on the ten or so journals—the top one-third of our 30 journals—that most frequently publish papers in each specialty.

We concentrate first on the algebra-algebraic geometry-topology set. The three specialties in this first set have many of the same journals in their respective top one-thirds. The *Illinois Journal of Mathematics, Quarterly Journal of Mathematics, American Journal of Mathematics, Compositio Mathematica, Annals of Mathematics,* and *Pacific Journal of Mathematics* are top third journals in two of the three fields. *Commentarii Mathematici Helvetici* and the *Pro-*

HIGHER ALGEBRA & GROUP THEORY	ALGEBRAIC GEOMETRY	TOPOLOGY
29% Math. Z.	40% Bull. Soc. Math. Fr.	29% Comment. Math. Helv.
26% Illinois J. Math.	39% Inventiones Math.	28% Illinois J. Math.
25% Quart. J. Math. Oxf.	32% Am. J. Math.	27% Michigan Math. J.
23% Compositio Math.	29% Compositio Math.	26% Dissertationes Math.
20% Pacific J. Math.	25% Math. USSR Izvestija	25% Ann. Math.
20% Bull. Soc. Math. Fr.	23% Ann. Math.	24% Quart. J. Math. Oxf.
18% Proc. Am. Math. Soc.	18% Duke Math. J.	22% Trans. Am. Math. Soc.
18% Comment. Math. Helv.	14% Acta Math. Uppsala	21% Am. J. Math.
17% Commun. Pure Appl. Math.	12% Comment. Math. Helv.	20% Proc. Am. Math. Soc.
16% Math. USSR Izvestija	10% Proc. Am. Math. Soc.	20% Pacific J. Math.
16% Advan. Math.		
15% Inventiones Math.	9% Pacific J. Math.	19% Compositio Math.
15% Ann. Math.	9% Trans. Am. Math.	17% Duke Math. J.
14% Trans. Am. Math. Soc.	9% Advan. Math.	16% Inventiones Math.
13% Duke Math. J.	9% Mich. Math. J.	12% Rocky Mtn. J. Math.
13% Rocky Mtn. J. Math.	8% Math. Z.	11% Acta Math. Uppsala
12% Am. J. Math.	7% Rocky Mtn. J. Math.	10% Math. Z.
10% Mich. Math. J.	7% Illinois J. Math.	10% Bull. Soc. Math. Fr.
10% Acta Math. Uppsala	7% Quart. J. Math. Oxf.	9% Indiana J. Math.
10% Dissertationes Math.	7% Indiana J. Math.	7% Math. USSR Izvestija
	7% Arch. Math. Basel	6% Advan. Math.
8% Siam. J. Appl. Math.	2% Commun. Pure Appl. Math.	2% J. Math. Anal. Appl.
8% Arch. Math. Basel	1% Quart. Appl. Math.	1% Siam J. Math. Anal.
3% Siam Rev.	1% Dissertationes Math.	1% Commun. Pure Appl. Math.
2% J. Math. Anal. Appl.	1% Siam Rev.	1% Z. Ang. Math. Phys.
2% Z. Angen. Math. Phys.	0% J. Math. Anal. Appl.	1% Arch. Math. Basel
1% Siam J. Math. Anal.	0% Siam J. Appl. Math.	0% Siam J. Appl. Math.
1% J. Inst. Math. Appl.	0% Siam J. Math. Anal.	0% J. Inst. Math. Appl.
0% Arch. Rational Mech. Anal.	0% Arch. Rational Math. Mech.	0% Arch. Rational Mech. Anal.
0% Indiana J. Math.	0% J. Inst. Math. Appl.	0% Quart. Appl. Math.
0% Quart. Appl. Math.	0% Z. Ang. Math. Physik	0% Siam Rev.

TABLE 1. Journals ranked by shares devoted to Algebra & Group Theory, Algebraic Geometry, and Topology. The top twenty journals for any one of these specialties tends to be the same as for the other two, with only their order of rank changed. Note the consistent representation of the more Applied journals among the "Worst" group.

ORDINARY DIFFERENTIAL EQUATIONS	PARTIAL DIFFERENTIAL EQUATIONS	APPLIED MATH. & OTHERS
20% Siam J. Math. Anal.	25% Commun. Pure Appl. Math.	84% J. Inst. Math. Appl.
15% J. Math. Anal. Appl.	22% Arch. Rational Mech. Anal.	72% Z. Ang. Math. Phys.
10% Siam. J. Appl. Math.	14% Indiana Math. J.	69% Quart. Appl. Math.
10% Siam Rev.	13% Siam J. Math. Anal.	64% Siam. J. Appl. Math.
8% Rocky Mtn. J. Math.	13% Z. Ang. Math. Phys.	61% Siam Rev.
8% Arch. Rational Mech. Anal.	13% Quart. Appl. Math.	51% Arch. Rational Mech. Anal.
8% Quart. Appl. Math.	11% Arch. Math. Basel	40% J. Math. Anal. Appl.
7% Quart. J. Math. Oxf.	8% J. Math. Anal. Appl.	26% Commun. Pure Appl. Math.
7% Commun. Pure Appl. Math.	8% Siam Rev.	23% Siam J. Math. Anal.
4% Proc. Am. Math. Soc.	7% Siam J. Appl. Math.	23% Rocky Mtn. J. Math.
4% Z. Ang. Math. Phys.		23% Advan. Math.
	6% Math. Z.	14% Dissertationes Math.
3% Pacific J. Math.	6% Acta Math. Uppsala	12% Indiana J. Math.
3% Trans. Am. Math. Soc.	5% Duke Math. J.	9% Math. Z.
3% Math USSR Izvestija	5% Rocky Mtn. J. Math.	9% Acta Math. Uppsala
3% J. Inst. Math. Appl.	4% Math. USSR Izvestija	9% Arch. Math. Basel
2% Math. Z.	4% Advan. Math.	7% Trans. Am. Math. Soc.
2% Indiana Math. J.	3% Trans. Am. Math. Soc.	7% Bull. Soc. Math. Fr.
2% Advan. Math.	2% Am. J. Math.	6% Pacific J. Math.
	2% Quart. J. Math. Oxf.	6% Math. USSR Izvestija
	2% J. Inst. Math. Appl.	6% Comment. Math. Helv.
	2% Ann. Math.	
		5% Proc. Am. Math. Soc.
1% Am. J. Math.	1% Pacific J. Math.	5% Inventiones Math.
1% Duke Math. J.	1% Illinois J. Math.	5% Duke J. Math.
1% Illinois J. Math.	1% Inventiones Math.	5% Ann. Math.
1% Inventiones Math.	1% Compositio Math.	4% Illinois J. Math.
1% Mich. Math. J.	1% Michigan Math. J.	4% Quart. J. Math. Oxf.
1% Comment. Math. Helv.	1% Bull. Soc. Math. Fr.	3% Am. J. Math.
1% Acta Math. Uppsala	1% Comment. Math. Helv.	2% Compositio Math.
1% Arch. Math. Basel	1% Dissertationes Math.	1% Michigan Math. J.
1% Dissertationes Math.		
0% Ann. Math.		
0% Compositio Math.		
0% Bull. Soc. Math. Fr.		

TABLE 2. Journals ranked by shares devoted to Ordinary Differential Equations, Partial Differential Equations, and Applied Mathematics. Note that the best journals for any one of these specialties tend to be the same as for the other two. Recall that these journals are the worst contributors to the fields of Table 1.

ceedings of the American Mathematical Society are top third journals for all three specialties in this set. In fact, the top two-thirds of the journals are almost the same—except for order—for any two of the three specialties. This implies a striking conclusion: the bottom third of journals for any one of the three specialties—algebra and group theory, algebraic geometry, topology—is likely to be the bottom third of "worst" group of journals for the other two as well.

This "worst" group provides evidence for the inverse relationship mentioned above. These journals form the top third of journals for the second set of specialties: ordinary differential equations, partial differential equations, and applied mathematics. The top third relationship is even stronger here than in the first set of specialties, for the following journals are in the top third of all three specialties of the second set: *Zeitschrift fur Angewandte Mathematik und Physik, Quarterly Journal of Applied Mathematics, SIAM Journal of Applied Mathematics, SIAM Review, Archive for Rational Mechanics and Analysis, Journal of Mathematical Analysis and Applications,* and *Communication on Pure and Applied Mathematics.* This collection of journals does not simply neglect algebra and group theory, algebraic geometry, and topology for the sake of a little more emphasis on the seven other specialty fields. Rather, as Table 2 suggests, this group concentrates on ordinary differential equations, partial differential equations, and applied mathematics.

These patterns of mutual emphasis and mutual devaluation are not accidental but rather reflect the current positions of pure mathematicians versus applied mathematicians on which mathematical specialties are worthwhile. Norwood states:

> Pure Mathematics asks, "What is? What different kinds of mathematical objects can exist? And how can we tell one when we have found one?"
>
> It would be a mistake to conclude that mathematicians necessarily care whether a new discovery has some practical application. Mathematicians do what they do because it is beautiful, interesting, challenging.[17]

Norwood might put almost all geometry and topology into this description, as well as much of algebra save some areas like matrix algebra and parts of group theory.

The attitude of the applied mathematicians is represented most strongly by Kline, a former topologist whose feelings for pure mathematics are clear:

> Blinded by a century of ever purer mathematics, most mathematicians have lost the skill to read the book of nature. They have turned to fields such as Abstract Algebra and Topology, to abstractions and generalizations such as Functional Analysis, to existence proofs for differential equations that are remote from applications, to axiomatizations of various bodies of thought, to arid brain games. Only a few still attempt to solve the most concrete problems, notably in Differential Equations and allied fields.[18]

While these two mathematicians cannot agree on which specialties are most valuable, they are likely to concur that pure workers dominate most general university mathematics departments and, thus, most general research journals. Norwood reports that much of statistics and computer science has broken away from mathematics (to become the responsibility of independent departments in larger academic institutions). Similarly, there have come to be many essentially independent journals devoted to these offshoots of mathematics. Kline reports that much of the best applied mathematics is done by other independent specialists as physicists and electrical engineers in their own departments and in some of their own journals. Still there are the minority applied mathematicians working in Pure Mathematics departments as well as closet purists at institutes of technology and schools of engineering. As fate and American library administration would have it, all these factions are often lumped together in the same science branch library with the same science librarian buying for them all.

Is there a way to determine quickly the pure or applied orientation of a journal, as a preliminary step in journal selection? The obvious marker is the word "applied" in the title or sponsoring agency's name. The Society for Industrial and Applied Mathematics (SIAM) and its journals were founded in strong reaction to the sense of isolation and perhaps even scorn felt by applied workers from the American Mathematical Society and its journals. In addition to SIAM journals, the "applied" marker works well for journals such as *Communications on Pure and Applied Mathematics, Zeitschrift fur Angewandte Mathematik und Physik,* and the *Journal of Mathematical Analysis and Applications.* But the suggested marker is scarcely infallible. The *Journal fur die Reine und Angewandte Mathematik* is strongly oriented toward pure mathematics. And journals such as the *Rocky Mountain Journal of Mathematics* and the *Indiana University Mathematics Journal* contain much applied mathematics while lacking the "applied" marker altogether.

The distribution of journals over the other four specialty fields (mathematical foundations, differential geometry, complex and harmonic analysis, real and abstract analysis) does not display the same degree of polarity of pure *vs.* applied journals as the two sets of three specialties discussed above. (See Table 3.)

Mathematical foundations is a predominantly pure area that produces papers for journals such as the *Quarterly Journal of Mathematics, Proceedings of the American Mathematical Society, Pacific Journal of Mathematics,* and *Mathematische Zeitschrift.* Interestingly, the top one-third of journals for this specialty also includes two SIAM journals, while the *Rocky Mountain Journal of Mathematics* is in the middle one-third. A reason for this is the increasing applicability of combinatorics. A few journals otherwise regarded as pure show extremely low interest in mathematical foundations: *Inventiones Mathematicae, Bulletin de la Societe Mathematique de France,* and the *American Journal of Mathematics.* Thus, in this specialty the pure versus applied polarity is not complete.

Differential geometry is also a predominantly pure field. Its top third journals include *Inventiones Mathematicae, Commentarii Mathematici Helvetici,* and *Annals of Mathematics.* Yet there are some surprising journals in the top third: *Communications on Pure and Applied Mathematics, Indiana University Journal of Mathematics,* and *Archive for Rational Mechanics and Analysis.* One reason for this intermingling between journals is that differential geometry can involve the use of differential equations. Also, there is a small vanguard of theoretical and mathematical physicists who hope to introduce this specialty to applications oriented audiences. The pure journals *(Illinois Journal of Mathematics, Arkiv for Mathematik, Quarterly Journal of Mathematics, Pacific Journal of Mathematics)* have surprisingly low representation in differential geometry. Again, polarization is not complete.

It is when we come to the enormous field of analysis that we see fairly cosmopolitan concerns from both pure and applied mathematicians. (See Table 4.) In the complex and harmonic analysis specialty it is still true that there is an academic flavor of predominantly pure journals in its top third, such as the *Michigan Mathema-*

PURE FOUNDATIONS, COMBINATORICS, & OTHERS	DIFFERENTIAL GEOMETRY
20% Dissertationes Math.	16% Inventiones Math.
11% Advan. Math.	15% Comment. Math. Helv.
9% Quart. J. Math. Oxf.	14% Ann. Math.
6% Proc. Am. Math. Soc.	13% Acta Math. Uppsala
6% Pacific J. Math.	10% Am. J. Math.
6% Trans. Am. Math. Soc.	9% Commun. Pure Appl. Math.
6% Math. Z.	8% Advan. Math.
6% Siam J. Appl. Math.	7% Indiana J. Math.
5% Siam Rev.	7% Duke Math. J.
	7% Arch. Rational Mech. Anal.
	7% Dissertationes Math.
4% Duke Math. J.	6% Math. USSR Izvestija
4% Compositio Math.	6% Mich. Math. J.
3% Rocky Mtn. J. Math.	6% Compositio Math.
3% Ann. Math.	5% Trans. Am. Math. Soc.
3% Acta Math. Uppsala	5% Bull. Soc. Math. Fr.
2% Illinois J. Math.	4% Proc. Am. Math. Soc.
2% Comment. Math. Helv.	4% Math. Z.
2% Math. USSR Izvestija	4% Rocky Mtn. J. Math.
2% Michigan Math. J.	
1% J. Math. Anal. Appl.	3% Illinois J. Math.
1% Siam J. Math. Anal.	3% Siam Rev.
1% Inventiones Math.	3% Arch. Math. Basel
1% Arch. Rational Math. Mech.	2% Quart. J. Math. Oxf.
1% Z. Ang. Math. Mech.	1% J. Math. Anal. Appl.
1% Bull. Soc. Math. Fr.	1% Pacific J. Math.
1% J. Inst. Math. Appl.	1% Siam J. Appl. Math.
0% Am. J. Math.	1% Quart. Appl. Math.
0% Indiana J. Math.	1% Z. Ang. Math. Phys.
0% Commun. Pure Appl. Math.	0% Siam J. Math. Anal.
0% Arch. Math. Basel	0% J. Inst. Math. Appl.
0% Quart. Appl. Math.	

TABLE 3. Journals ranked by shares devoted to Mathematical Foundations and Differential Geometry. While pure journals predominate in the upper groupings, some applied journals do well.

COMPLEX AND HARMONIC ANALYSIS	REAL AND ABSTRACT ANALYSIS
21% Michigan Math. J.	42% Indiana J. Math.
21% Arch. Math. Basel	39% Arch. Math. Basel
19% Acta Math. Uppsala	37% Siam J. Math. Anal.
14% Comment. Math. Helv.	27% J. Math. Anal. Appl.
9% Pacific J. Math.	25% Proc. Am. Math. Soc.
9% Trans. Am. Math. Soc.	25% Pacific J. Math.
9% Duke Math. J.	24% Michigan Math. J.
	23% Math. USSR Izvestija
	22% Trans. Am. Math. Soc.
	22% Illinois J. Math.
7% Proc. Am. Math. Soc.	21% Duke Math. J.
7% Math. Z.	18% Math. Z.
7% Indiana J. Math.	18% Rocky Mtn. J. Math.
7% Math. USSR Izvestija	18% Dissertationes Math.
7% Rocky Mtn. J. Math.	17% Quart. J. Math. Oxf.
6% Illinois J. Math.	17% Advan. Math.
5% Commun. Pure Appl. Math.	15% Am. J. Math.
4% J. Math. Anal. Appl.	15% Bull. Soc. Math. Fr.
4% Arch. Rational Mech. Anal.	15% Acta Math. Uppsala
4% Am. J. Math.	13% Compositio Math.
4% Ann. Math.	
3% Siam J. Math. Anal.	9% Ann. Math.
3% Inventiones Math.	9% Siam Rev.
3% Advan. Math.	8% J. Inst. Math. Appl.
3% Z. Ang. Math. Phys.	7% Arch. Rational Mech. Anal.
3% Compositio Math.	7% Commun. Pure Appl. Math.
2% Quart. J. Math. Oxf.	6% Quart. Appl. Math.
2% Bull. Soc. Math. Fr.	4% Inventiones Math.
1% J. Inst. Math. Appl.	3% Siam J. Appl. Math.
1% Quart. Appl. Math.	3% Comment. Math. Helv.
1% Dissertationes Math.	3% Z. Ang. Math. Phys.
0% Siam J. Appl. Math.	
0% Siam Rev.	

TABLE 4. Journals ranked by shares devoted to Complex and Harmonic Analysis, and Real and Abstract Analysis. Both pure and applied journals regularly feature Analysis, with pure journals leading in the first specialty and applied in the second.

tical Journal, Arkiv for Mathematik, Acta Mathematica, and *Commentarii Mathematici Helvetici.* However, those journals noted for leaning to more applicable fields all make a good showing in the second third of complex and harmonic analysis: *Indiana University Journal of Mathematics, Rocky Mountain Journal of Mathematics, Communications on Pure and Applied Mathematics, Archive for Rational Mechanics and Analysis,* the *Journal of Mathematical Analysis and Applications.* The other specialty of analysis is real and abstract analysis, and its top third is dominated by the journals in the second third of complex and harmonic analysis, plus the *SIAM Journal on Mathematical Analysis.* Also in the top third of real and abstract analysis are the purer *Proceedings* and *Transactions of the American Mathematical Society,* the *Pacific Journal of Mathematics, Michigan Mathematical Journal,* and *Duke Mathematical Journal.* This joint interest in Real and Abstract Analysis is not accidental, for analysis is the last frequently used meeting ground of pure and applied mathematics, a fact acknowledged inside the cover of every issue of the *SIAM Journal on Mathematical Analysis:*

> [This journal] contains research articles on the part of Analysis which bridges pure mathematics and numerical, physical, and engineering applications. Topics include Asymptotic Analysis, Generalized Functions, Harmonic Analysis, Integral Transforms, and Special Functions.

This wide range of papers in analysis leaves the librarian in a good news/bad news situation. The good news is that almost any journal, except some extremely pure and some extremely applied journals, is likely to have some analysis content, and so the chances of making a radical selection mistake is rare in this specialty. The bad news is that the librarian must buy a lot of journals to get the same level of coverage in analysis as might be gotten in less diffused fields requiring only a few strongly biased journals.

PRACTICALITY AND RELIABILITY

Reasonable questions can be asked about our approach. Are the time and expense worth the kind of selection data gathered? Must all eight years of a journal's content be studied? Are the underlying subject emphases of these journals likely to remain the same after an analysis is completed?

In the first instance, the task is so uncomplicated that the analysis of a journal can be assigned to a clerk and completed in several hours. It is not even necessary to have immediate access to a complete run of the journal. The clerk can work from tables of contents obtained via interlibrary loan. Alternatively, the procedure can be done online without using even the printed tables of contents. For our paper we analyzed eight years of *Zeitschrift fur Angewandte Mathematik und Physik* using MATHFILE, the online counterpart of *MR*. Compare our online investment of 27 minutes and $27.50 with the journal's current annual subscription rate of $262.

In the second instance, the time span of papers to be studied in a journal cannot be specified uniformly for all journals. Patterns of subject emphasis can be determined reliably only when enough articles are examined. As a rule of thumb, we suggest that two years of a journal, or 200 articles, whichever supplied fewer articles, should be sufficient.

In the third instance, the stability of subject analysis cannot be guaranteed, but there are three reassuring factors. First, consider that many of these journals have loyal clienteles who would be unlikely to support radical subject shifts. A good example would be the membership of SIAM, which worked so hard to establish journals emphasizing its particular interests. Second, the stability of editorial boards favor slow change. Many editors appear to serve quite long terms, and they tend to attract papers from authors who understand what subjects are likely to interest those editors. Even the selection of new editors is a gradual process. Candidates for an editorship are likely to include authors who have shown interest in the journal through their pattern of successful manuscript submissions appropriate to the journal's subject. Third, consider the rather tardy appearance of papers in many of these journals. For example, papers appearing in the January 1983 issue of *Annals of Mathematics* were submitted as long ago as January 1981. Many journals seem to have up to two years of backlogs of already accepted articles. Therefore, the evidence of an unlikely radical shift might take a couple of years to appear in print.

A FINAL WORD

While the authors feel that for the particular circumstances described our method offers advantages over the consulting of standard buying guides or the use of citation indexing data, we suggest that a combination of all these methods is likely to make for the most informative selection decisions.

REFERENCES

1. See: Hirsch, Morris W. *Differential geometry.* New York: Springer Verlag; 1976: p. 169.
2. Stankus, Tony; Schlessinger, Rashelle; Schlessinger, Bernard S. English language trends in German basic science journals: a potential collection tool. *Science & Technology Libraries.* 1(3): 55-66; 1981 Spring.
3. Stankus, Tony. Collection development: journals for biochemists. *Special Collections.* 1(2): 51-74; 1981 Winter. (See particularly the discussion on pages 57-60 and the summation at the bottom of Table 2.)
4. Stankus, Tony; Rice, Barbara. Handle with care: use and citation data for science journal management. *Collection Management.* 4(1/2): 95-110; 1982 Spring/Summer.
5. Garfield, Eugene. *Citation indexing–its theory and application in science, technology, and humanities.* New York: Wiley; 1979: Chapter 9.
6. Garfield, Eugene. Highly cited papers in mathematics. Part 1. Pure mathematics. Part 2. Applied mathematics. *Essays of an information scientist.* Philadelphia: Institute for Scientific Information; 1977: p. 504-13.
7. Garfield, Eugene. Journal citation studies. 36. Pure and applied mathematics journals: what they cite and vice-versa. *Current Contents.* 23(15): 5-13; 1982 April 12.
8. See: Katz, Bill; Katz, Linda Sternberg. *Magazines for libraries.* 4th ed. New York: Bowker; 1982: p. 633-41.
9. Malinowsky, H. Robert; Richardson, Jeanne M. *Science and engineering literature: a guide to reference sources.* 3d ed. Littleton, CO: Libraries Unlimited; 1980: Chapter 4.
10. Chen, Ching-Chih. *Scientific and technical information sources.* Cambridge, MA: MIT Press; 1977: p. 359-360.
11. Subramanyam, Krishna. *Scientific and technical information resources.* New York: Marcel Dekker; 1981: Chapter 18.
12. Pemberton, John E. *How to find out in mathematics.* Oxford: Pergamon; 1970.
13. Dorling, A. R. *Use of mathematical literature.* London: Butterworths; 1977: Chapter 2.
14. Dick, Elie M. *Current information sources in mathematics: an annotated guide to books and periodicals, 1960-72.* Littleton, CO: Libraries Unlimited; 1973: p. 240-51.
15. Kusma, Taissa T. Computerization of *Mathematical Reviews* into MATHFILE. *Science & Technology Libraries.* 3(1): 49-62; 1982 Fall.
16. Diodato, Virgil P. Author indexing. *Special Libraries.* 72(4): 361-9; 1981 October.
17. Norwood, Rick. In abstract terrain. *The Sciences.* 22(9): 12-18; 1982 December.
18. Kline, Morris. *Mathematics: the loss of certainty.* New York: Oxford; 1980: Chapter XIII.

Appendix A.

Correspondence Between Specialty Categories and
Mathematical Reviews Classification Codes

Stankus/Diodato Specialty Categories	MR Classification Codes
1. Mathematical Foundations	00 through 08
2. Algebra and Group Theory	10,15,16,17,18,20
3. Algebraic Geometry	12,13,14,32
4. Complex and Harmonic Analysis	30,31,43
5. Ordinary Differential Equations	34
6. Partial Differential Equations	35
7. Real and Abstract Analysis	26,28,40,41,42 44,45,46,47,56
8. Differential Geometry	53,58
9. Topology	22,54,55,57
10. Applied Mathematics	all others

Appendix B.

The Number of Articles per Specialty in Each Journal, 1972-1979

	Stankus/Diodato Category										
	1	2	3	4	5	6	7	8	9	10	Tot
Acta Mathematica (Uppsala)	4	14	20	27	1	9	21	19	16	13	144
Advances in Mathematics	38	57	30	11	8	15	61	28	21	82	351
American Journal of Mathematics	2	54	142	18	5	10	69	43	93	12	448
Annals of Mathematics	10	51	79	13	1	5	30	46	86	17	338

Appendix B. (Continued)

The Number of Articles per Specialty in Each Journal, 1972-1979

	Stankus/Diodato Category										
	1	2	3	4	5	6	7	8	9	10	Tot
Archive for Rational Mechanics and Analysis	3	2	1	20	36	101	30	29	0	228	450
Arkiv for Mathematik (Basel)	0	11	10	31	1	16	57	5	1	13	145
Bulletin de la Societe Mathematique de France	1	34	69	4	0	2	25	8	17	12	172
Commentarii Mathematici Helvetici	7	55	38	42	2	2	10	47	89	18	310
Communications on Pure and Applied Mathematics	1	42	5	13	17	61	17	23	2	63	244
Compositio Mathematica	11	62	79	7	1	3	36	16	52	5	272
Dissertationes Mathematicae	15	7	1	1	1	1	13	5	19	10	73
Duke Mathematical Journal	22	71	95	47	4	29	112	35	92	26	533
Illinois Journal of Mathematics	9	114	31	27	4	5	94	13	122	16	435
Indiana University Mathematics Journal	2	16	27	45	16	91	280	49	59	80	665
Inventiones Mathematicae	4	83	219	16	3	5	25	88	89	27	559
Journal of Mathematical Analysis and Applications	24	33	4	66	273	151	481	23	30	722	1807

Appendix B. (Continued)

The Number of Articles per Specialty in Each Journal, 1972-1979

	Stankus/Diodato Category										
	1	2	3	4	5	6	7	8	9	10	Tot
Journal of the Institute of Mathematics and its Applications	1	4	1	4	14	8	34	0	1	355	422
Mathematics of the USSR - Izvestija	7	76	120	33	16	20	108	30	34	29	473
Mathematische Zeitschrift	77	351	94	89	25	78	226	55	124	111	1230
Michigan Mathematical Journal	6	33	30	72	3	3	80	19	91	3	340
Pacific Journal of Mathematics	150	481	205	221	68	28	610	20	478	138	2399
Proceedings of the American Mathematical Society	243	736	399	304	151	82	1042	173	842	213	4185
Quarterly of Applied Mathematics	1	0	3	2	19	30	14	3	0	156	228
Quarterly Journal of Mathematics (Oxford)	34	91	24	9	26	9	62	7	85	13	360
Rocky Mountain Journal of Mathematics	11	58	32	33	37	24	80	16	53	101	445
SIAM Journal on Applied Mathematics	51	68	4	2	83	57	28	7	4	549	853
SIAM Journal on Mathematical Analysis	7	6	2	23	142	95	264	3	4	167	713

Appendix B. (Continued)

The Number of Articles per Specialty in Each Journal, 1972-1979

	Stankus/Diodato Category										
	1	2	3	4	5	6	7	8	9	10	Tot
SIAM Review	8	5	1	0	18	13	16	6	0	105	172
Transactions of the American Mathematical Society	139	327	200	209	67	61	493	121	489	154	2260
Zeitschrift fur Angewandte Mathematik und Physik	3	6	0	8	12	40	10	3	2	222	306
Total	891	2948	1965	1397	1054	1054	4428	940	2995	3660	21332

Pharmacy Faculty Members' Exposure to Current Periodicals

Wendell A. Guy

ABSTRACT. An analysis of the journals routed to and received personally by a pharmacy college faculty revealed that widely held areas of interest, memberships in organizations, and specialty interests were important factors in determining which journals were most widely seen. The faculty widely held interests in general medical, clinical pharmacy, and "general" pharmacy periodicals. Each faculty subgroup had distinct interests in certain journals, few of which were on more than one of the subgroups' most viewed journals list.

The existence of a periodical routing system at the Arnold and Marie Schwartz College of Pharmacy (Brooklyn, New York) made it possible to determine the faculty's exposure to journals and periodicals.

The system routes 208 periodicals which cover all areas of pharmacy, plus a few selected medical and scientific journals. The journal exposure of thirty five faculty members, both teaching faculty and administrators, is reported. All the faculty members are involved with the last three years of the pharmacy curriculum which is known as "professional studies," as opposed to the liberal arts and basic science studies which comprise the first two years of the curriculum.

To make this study more complete, faculty members were asked which pharmacy, medical and scientific periodicals they personally receive, either through subscriptions, via memberships in a society,

---

Wendell A. Guy is Director, Learning Resources Center, Dowling College, Oakdale, NY 11769.

or on a free basis. The term "most seen" will be used throughout this study as it was not possible to determine whether the periodicals received by the faculty members were actually read.

The 35 faculty members placed 1,120 requests for journals through the routing system. This averaged 32 journals per faculty member. The faculty members also received 186 journals personally. This averaged 5.31 journals per faculty member.

Table 1 reports the list of most seen journals. Column #1 ranks

TABLE 1

Rank order listing of the 26 most seen periodicals:

#1 Rank	#2 Total Seen		#3 Routed	#4 Personal
1	26	American Journal of Pharmaceutical Education	8	18
2	22	American Pharmacy	6	16
3/	20	Journal of the American Medical Association	18	2
4	20	New England Journal of Medicine	14	6
5	19	Journal of Pharmaceutical Sciences	8	11
6/	18	American Druggist	15	3
7	18	U.S. Pharmacist	9	9
8	17	Clinical Pharmacology and Therapeutics	15	2
9/	16	American Journal of Hospital Pharmacy	7	9
10/	16	Drug Intelligence and Clinical Pharmacy	15	1
11/	16	Drug Therapy	14	2
12	16	Medical Letter on Drugs and Therapuetics	14	2
13	15	Journal of Clinical Pharmacology	12	3
14/	14	Drug Interactions Newsletter	14	0
15	14	Pharmacy Times	12	2
16/	13	Canadian Journal of Pharmaceutical Sciences	13	0
17/	13	Drug Nutrient Interactions	13	0
18	13	Journal of Pharmacy and Pharmacology	13	0
19/	12	Clinical Pharmacokinetics	12	0
20/	12	Drug Topics	12	0
21/	12	Journal of Pharmacology and Experimental Therapeutics	12	0
22	12	Pediatric Pharmacology	12	0
23/	11	INPHARMA	11	0
24	11	Pharmacological Reviews	11	0
25/	10	Lippincott's Hospital Pharmacy	8	2
26	10	Medicinal Research Reviews	10	0

Note: A "/" indicates a tie for ranking.

the combined total, seen both through routing and through personal receipt. The most widely seen journal is the *American Journal of Pharmaceutical Education* with 26 faculty members receiving it. This, and the second most seen journal, *American Pharmacy*, are both received automatically through memberships in national pharmacy organizations. Both of these journals will be classified as general pharmacy periodicals. The first deals with pharmacy as an institution and the second is written for all kinds of pharmacists. Most pharmacy periodicals are related to some specialized aspect of either pharmacy science or pharmacy practice.

Tied for third and fourth places are two prestigious general medical journals: *JAMA* and the *New England Journal of Medicine*. Their placing so high on the list reflects the keen interest among pharmacy faculty in medicine and pharmacy's continual close relationship with medicine.

Table 2 reports the number of periodicals in each subject area for the 26 most seen journals. While the most numerous category is pharmacy science, only two of these journals appear in the upper half of the list.

Both available clinical pharmacy periodicals published in the United States appear in the upper half of the list. This reflects the wide interest in patient-oriented pharmacy, a relatively new approach to pharmacy practice. Most of the available pharmacy practice/commerce magazines appear on the list, reflecting the continued popularity of the traditional drug store approach to pharmacy. However, only one of these magazines appears on the upper half of the list.

Four relatively new periodicals are on the list: *Drug Interactions Newsletter; Drug Nutrient Interactions, Pediatric Pharmacology* and *Medicinal Research Reviews*. There is a widespread interest by faculty members in receiving periodicals which have just started being published.

Column #3, on Table 1, reports the number of faculty members receiving a periodical through the routing system. Column #4 reports the numbers of each journal being received personally. The four most received journals are all related to a membership in a national pharmacy organization. The fifth most personally received journal is *Science*, which did not rank high enough to appear on the combined list. Eight faculty members receive this journal through membership in a non-pharmacy national organization.

The combined list reveals the journal exposure of the entire facul-

TABLE 2

Classification of most seen periodicals by subject:

Subject	
Pharmacy science	12
Pharmacy practice/commerce	3
Drug oriented	3
Medical periodicals	3
Clinical Pharmacy	2
General Pharmacy	2
Hospital Pharmacy	2

ty as a whole. The appearance of a journal on this list is related to how many faculty members there are with similar academic, professional and research interests. The faculty is also composed of subgroups, each with interests of its own. Three such subgroups are the pharmacy practice subgroup; the pharmacy related science subgroup; and the pharmaceutical science subgroup.

The pharmacy practice subgroup includes thirteen professors whose major interests are community, hospital and clinical pharmacy; pharmacy law; drug information; pharmacy administration; and biostatistics. These professors placed a total of 417 requests for routing, or 32.07 per professor. They received personally 60 periodicals, or 4.6 per professor. (See Table 3 for this group's most viewed periodicals.) Included here are both clinical pharmacy and both hospital pharmacy periodicals as well as all of the pharmacy practice/commerce magazines. None of the pharmacy science journals is present.

The pharmacy related science subgroup contains twelve faculty whose major interests include pharmacology, toxicology, pharmacognosy, biochemistry, and medicinal chemistry. This subgroup placed 422 requests for routing, or 35.16 per professor. They personally received 74 journals, or 6.2 per professor. Their most seen journals are reported on Table 3. They are very interested in pharmacology. Two of these journals, *Science* and *Toxicology and Applied Pharmacology* did not rank high enough to appear on the combined list. While both medical journals appear on this list, none of the pharmacy practice (clinical, hospital or pharmacy practice/commerce) journals appear on their list.

The third subgroup, the pharmaceutical science subgroup, consists of ten professors whose major interests include biopharmaceutics, cosmetic science, industrial pharmacy, and physical pharmacy. This subgroup placed a total of 281 requests for routing or 28.1 per professor. They personally received 52 journals, or 5.2 per professor. Their most seen journals appear on Table 3. Four of these journals did not rank high enough to appear on the combined list. These include: *Drug and Cosmetic Industry; Drug Development and Industrial Pharmacy; Journal of the Society of Cosmetic Chemists;* and the *International Journal of Cosmetic Science.* There are no medical, pharmacy practice, or pharmacology journals on this list. While their list is the most distinctive, they have the least amount of influence on the combined list because they are the smallest subgroup.

In looking at these three lists, it is evident that no one journal appears on all three lists. Five journals, however, do appear on more than one list. *AJPE* and *JAMA* appear on the pharmacy practice and pharmacy related science lists. *American Pharmacy* and *DICP* appear on the pharmacy practice and pharmaceutical sciences lists. *JPharmSci* appears on the pharmacy related sciences and the pharmaceutical sciences lists.

TABLE 3

Ranked lists of most seen journals for the three subgroups:

Pharmacy Practice	Pharmacy Related Sciences	Pharmaceutical Science
1 AJPE	1/ J. Clinical Pharmacology	1/ American Pharmacy
	2 NEJM	2 JPharmSci
2 USPharmacist		
	3/ AJPE	3 Canadian JPharmSci
3/ American Druggist	4 Pharmacological Reviews	
4 Pharmacy Times		4/ Drug & Cosmetic Industry
	5/ JAMA	5/ Drug Development & Industrial Pharmacy
5/ American Pharmacy	6/ JPharmSci	
6 Lippincotts Hospital Pharmacy	7/ J. Pharmacology & Experimental Therapeutics	6 JSocCosmetic Chemists
	8 Toxicology & Applied Pharmacology	7/ DI&CP
7/ AJHP		8 IntJCosmetic Sci
8/ DI&CP		
9/ Drug Topics		
10 JAMA		

Note: A "/" mark indicates a tie for a ranking.

CONCLUSIONS

This study has shown:

1. Members of a pharmacy faculty routinely review a surprisingly large number of journals.
2. Widely shared interests in clinical pharmacy, general medicine, and "general" pharmacy exist among the faculty. These interests place certain journals high on a combined list of most seen periodicals.
3. Memberships in national organizations play an important role in determining that a select number of periodicals are distributed to large numbers of faculty members.
4. Subgroups of faculty members have their own distinct interests which becomes evident when their separate lists of most seen journals are determined. Only a few journals appear on more than one of the subgroups' most viewed journals lists.
5. In comparison to the number of requests for routing, the number of periodicals being received personally is relatively small. Most of these are being received through a membership in an organization.

Publishing—A View on Science/Technology Information (STI) Transfer

David L. Staiger

ABSTRACT. A viewpoint is given on the breakup of classic science/technology information (STI) publishing functions that are accelerated by advances in technology. The publisher value-added function is stressed for conventional publishing. By-the-hit marketing is emphasized for low readership material.

Publishing starts with the author and ends with the reader. All that transpires between these two points is part of a delivery system that ultimately is judged by its effectiveness in making this connection. When approached from this viewpoint the word "publishing" loses clarity of definition and at best can be considered a subset of information transfer. This defocusing has been particularly evident in the Science/Technology information (STI) area.

ROLE PLAYING

In the process of making the connection between author and reader, two functions emerge: a delivery system and the value-added function. The delivery system covers a lot of the mechanics and includes finding the right reader for the author—commonly called marketing. The value-added function takes several forms, such as accuracy, completeness, clarity and distillation.

There has been a progressive break-up of the functions that were

---

David L. Staiger is Staff Director, Publishing Services, Institute of Electrical and Electronics Engineers, 345 E. 47th Street, New York, NY 10017. He has the MS degree in Aeronautical Engineering from Rensselaer Polytechnic Institute. He has been involved in technical publishing for more than 25 years.

© 1983 by The Haworth Press, Inc. All rights reserved.

previously attributed to a classic publisher. Not too many years ago the publisher arranged for all the steps between the author and reader. In practice he either did them himself, paid to have them done, or worked closely with others such as bookstores and libraries.

Using the printing industry as an example of how technology can precipitate a "break-up," consider the impact of offset printing. Composition need not be done at the same geographical location as printing, as was once practically required with letterpress printing and hot metal typesetting. This made it possible for the publisher to shop around for both functions independent of each other. The printer then had to reevaluate his position. First he had to decide if he could compete with companies that specialized in just printing or just typesetting. Next he had to determine how many customers wanted to deal with just one source of supply—and how much they would pay for this convenience. Finally, in cases where he was just doing the printing, he had to develop a new method of customer contact. It is in this last case that the impact of technology is difficult to evaluate. The printer's relationship with a customer used to be a combination of bottom-line bidding and keeping the editor happy with day-to-day relationships concerned primarily with typesetting. Once the day-to-day relationships moved over to an independent typesetter, a new series of contacts was needed and they required a different type of handling. In practice these relationships shifted from editors to publishers or business managers/purchasing agents. This cut off another avenue of information—advance knowledge of what new business was coming up. Editors were a better source of this information.

Compounding the printing-typesetting relationships was the fact that offset printing stimulated new mechanisms of typesetting. The person who went into just this business didn't inherit the old front end of customer relationships from the printer. Rather he found that he could be in competition with his own customer. The new typesetting technology was adaptable to a business office environment and the economics of capital investment was within the customer's finances. It wasn't much later, as the customer understood more about the process, that substitutions for typesetting were accepted which range from a good typewriter to the current vogue of word processing.

The analogy I would like to make here is that originally the printer viewed the new technology of offset printing as an improvement in manufacturing efficiency. Publishers are faced with changes that are far more complex than a single improvement in printing press efficiency and can look forward to a series of difficult-to-predict conditions. Librarians are in the same boat.

BREAK-UP FACTORS

What then are some of the break-up factors from the publisher's viewpoint—particularly the publishers in the science and technology information field? Viewing them from a business standpoint, the following situation exists.

A main change has been in the "science" of business. Technical information has been moving in-house. Much of the engineering, and, in larger corporations, a lot of the science, is done within corporate walls and is considered corporate property. The transfer of this information doesn't involve the classic publisher except downstream when the information goes public. It is estimated that an engineer gets about 10% of the information he needs to do his job from public (published) sources with the rest coming from in-house documentation and peer contact, the customer, and vendors. A not dissimilar situation occurs in government, either through security restrictions or funding arrangements. While funding reaches into the universities, at least in this area there is a strong motivation to go public at the earliest possible date. There is little that the STI publisher can do about the developments that are changing business except to recognize that they probably outweigh all the local changes, like printing technologies.

Author relations would get second place on a list of long range critical break-up factors. The key here is that STI authors earn their living elsewhere and being an author is not their primary concern—in fact it is the "elsewhere" that makes them valuable as an author in the first place. Authors are getting smarter about the publishing mechanism and are already exercising options—not dissimilar to a customer getting into typesetting in the above printing example. Publishers are now engaged in a program to get authors to send in their manuscripts in a standard machine-readable form. This would make more money for the publisher by reducing his costs. It is just a short step to the point where an author will be able to emulate the graphic quality standards used in publishing and have some automated copy editing support to boot. Add to this the fact that some authors, particularly on the West Coast, have already found that they can get soft covered books manufactured by photocopy houses and you have the beginnings of a do-it-yourself author/publisher community. The relationship with the STI author has been bounded by the economics of the publisher. They have been dictated by the marketplace for STI information, with low readership being the limiting factor. The beginnings of an author/publisher role are just an indication that these limits are being stretched. The conventional method of making low readership information available has been such things as journals and libraries. The journal packages together items that wouldn't be economically viable if published separately. The libraries have been looked to as "funding" agencies to further extend the marketplace, technically as a mechanism for multiple use. From the author's standpoint it becomes progressively more difficult to be published, and most authors already donate their time for their writing efforts. There will be a limiting point for this type of relationship under conventional publishing concepts.

The growth of information available is in itself a break-up factor. The Institute of Electrical and Electronics Engineers (IEEE) is an example of the impact of this growth factor. The organization has divided itself into over 30 technical "societies," each handling a segment of the information that used to be covered by two organizations. The compounding of this effect has led to a new industry that is referred to as networking. Now millions of technical items are made known to the reader by these networks and the last part of the printing example comes into play. The publisher loses contact with the reader just as the printer lost contact with the editor. Libraries are the earlier part of this disconnection and the electronic networks are accelerating the process. Feedback is an essential part of the publishing process just as in any other industry. Progressive loss of feedback puts further economic boundaries on the range of published material. It isn't enough to know what's needed (selling), you also have to know why—and this is the role of feedback.

Thus the role of the publisher is becoming diluted and limited in the basic author-reader chain. Technical progress is serving to find alternate paths for information where the publishing mechanism is stressed by the environment in which it is embedded. The emphasis is on the environmental factors rather than the details of the technology for it is these stresses that accelerate the application of technology.

VALUE-ADDED FUNCTION

The evaluation and distillation of information is a "value-added" role of a publisher. The problems of running a distribution system mentioned above assumed that the author/reader connection was a mechanical one. The value-added function of a publisher addresses a fundamental problem in this connection, the fact that the author and reader have different objectives. One is telling what he knows and the other is looking for help. The publisher acts as a translator between the two by applying a value judgment to the information. This judgment may act to clarify the author's presentation or it may combine many people's work into one—commonly called textbooks, reference books, tutorials, etc. In any case it functions to improve the transfer of information. It is here that I feel the function of a publisher is coming into sharper focus. The loss of control of the mechanics of publication should cause publishers to look more carefully at the value-added role.

At this point a distinction should be drawn between commercial and not-for-profit publishers. The commercial publisher actively seeks out authors that will have a high probability of "value-added" manuscripts. A prime example is the textbook area. They do this because it is good business. Not-for-profit publishers (societies and universities) tend to keep wide open doors for authors and apply a quality control (peer review) to the author's work, but they do not necessarily seek out authors to fill specific readers' needs. An offsetting factor for professional societies is that they have independent means of communicating with a wide group of readers via membership in the society.

MARKETING

When the changes in technology get finished supplying alternate ways of responding to the pressures applied by the information environment, what will we have to sell—and how will we sell it? I believe we have to learn to sell by the hit and the package.

Publishers who supply a high level of value-added products will keep corresponding high levels of readership and will continue to sell packages of information to readers. Call such products books or magazines if you like, functionally they will represent material that has been distilled, clarified, and translated into reader terms. The size and diversity of information will make it impossible to package everything so this will lead to a "hit" marketplace where the reader can go shopping for the pieces he needs—and will act as his own packager.

The newer "hit" marketplace is already with us in the form of photocopying or publish-on-demand techniques. New technology will only accelerate this demand, not create it. The challenge to the publisher is to develop a way to encompass this new marketplace. The database people learned how to do it through such techniques as connect-time, CPU time, items hit or printed, etc. Many of the same organizations started with packages called indexes and still do a fair amount of this business.

This "hit" marketplace will allow publishers to cross over into the areas that are presently artificially supported. Authors can be connected up to readers in a much more realistic way with a hit technology. Even the publishing economics may turn out to be better than we think as one item of information will cost more but fewer will have to be bought by the reader.

THE LIBRARY

Where does the library fit into this picture—I wish I knew. According to my value-added approach, they look more like a future publisher than I find it comfortable to contemplate. They already are very close to the publish-on-demand role. Currently libraries are supplying a form of peer review to the information that comes out of the online networks. In a roundabout way they are in the acquisitions business. Then what might be different between a library of the future and a publisher of the future? The key point probably is one of librarians wanting to be in the information business rather than the information service business. I'll know this has happened when a library stock is on the big board of the NYSE.

SPECIAL PAPER

The In-House Translator: An Overlooked Specialist

Patricia E. Newman

ABSTRACT. Describes the functions and qualifications of in-house translators, comparing their work with that of contract translators. Ways in which in-house translators aid library staffs are discussed.

We are no longer in the Atomic Age, the experts tell us, but rather in the Information Age, and the information specialist is expected to provide a bewildering variety of services to the patrons who flock to the library. Library schools teach the basics, workshops teach on-line searching, and journals fill in the gaps with what-every-librarian-should-know articles, but it is simply impossible for a librarian to be all things to all patrons. Even small libraries are seeing a trend toward specialization. One often-overlooked specialist who can be of immense aid to both librarian and patron is the in-house translator, the resident linguistic consultant.

This article will explore the various ways in which in-house translators fit into the information services provided by a science and technology library and the advantages and disadvantages to the company of using in-house translators instead of or in addition to outside

---

Patricia Newman is the in-house technical translator at Sandia National Laboratories, Albuquerque, New Mexico 87185. She received a BS in Electrical Engineering, a BA in Modern Languages from the University of New Mexico and translates Russian, German, French and Spanish. She is currently a Director of the American Translators Association and is accredited by ATA for translation from Russian and German to English.

© 1983 by The Haworth Press, Inc. All rights reserved.

services. We'll start with the ways in which in-house translators can help the patrons, and then we'll look at the ways in which they can help the library staff.

NATURE AND FUNCTIONS

The best way to begin is to define the terms. An in-house translator is an employee of the company, part of whose primary job responsibility is translation. Many combine translation with other responsibilities, such as technical writing, library science, chemistry or cataloging, but to qualify for the title of in-house translators, they must spend part of their time during regular working hours translating.

In-house translators come in a variety of models, and a company must be judicious in its selection, since someone who is an ideal in-house translator for one company is unsuitable for another. An electrical engineer who reads Russian, German, and French might be ideal for Sandia National Laboratories but unqualified for a job at Eastman Kodak, for example.

Contract translators are not considered employees of the company but rather contractors who work on a job-at-a-time basis. Contract translators include both free-lance translators and translation bureaus, which may or may not employ free-lances as subcontractors.[1]

Now we turn to a description of the company in need of translation services. We assume that our hypothetical company is a research and development concern that employs enough scientists and engineers to generate a significant number of translation requests. Chances are that they participate in meetings with foreign counterparts. The most requested languages are Russian, German, French, Spanish and Japanese, with a sprinkling of others, and most of the requests are for translation from foreign languages into English.[2] There is a special library on the premises, and the librarians are responsible for all information services, from selective dissemination of information to on-line searches to foreign documents. How do in-house translators fit into this picture?

The conventional image patrons and librarians alike have of translation is what is called the formal translation. The foreign document is sent to a translator, and after a wait that ranges from long to intolerable, the translator returns a copy of the foreign document with an English translation and a bill for services rendered. As far as patron and librarian can tell, translations differ only in price, time, and readability. Can in-house translators take over all the requests that used to be sent to contract translators and do them faster, cheaper and better? Can in-house translators leap tall buildings in a single bound?

While in-house translators can certainly produce formal translations of documents in languages they know, it is unreasonable to expect them to know every language and to translate equally well into and out of foreign languages. Some work must still be sent outside to contract translators, and the question is then how such a limited specialist can benefit the company. The answers are quality, flexibility, availability, and familiarity.

The quality of a translation depends on three things: linguistic knowledge (you can't translate it if you can't read the foreign language), subject knowledge (you can't translate it well if you can't understand the subject), and writing ability (you can't translate it well if your reader can't understand your English).

Translators, either in-house or contract, are usually selected for their linguistic capabilities; it is obviously ridiculous to send a German document to a translator who reads only French. Most good translators, however, will also claim a subject speciality, realizing what most patrons don't, namely that every field of science and technology has its own sublanguage.[3] In-house translators are by necessity specialists in whatever field in which their employer is interested; consequently the quality and consistency of their translations should be high. In addition, they have access to the company library, which specializes in these subject areas, and to the patron who requested the translation, who should be an expert in the subject matter.

In-house translators offer a flexibility in informal translations that contract translators find it difficult to match. For example, although the formal translation is the general rule, many patrons are discerning enough to realize that, just like members of the opposite sex, a document may have an alluring cover with very little of interest underneath. It is easy to drop in on in-house translators and ask them to scan through a document to see if it contains anything of interest. They can be asked to write abstracts of papers, make marginal notes of the contents as they read through them, or make rough-draft translations in a hurry. They can even dictate rough translations into a tape recorder, which the user may simply listen to without waiting for a transcription. This is what is meant by flexibility.

Availability is simply being close at hand and having unusual knowledge and skills to offer. Contract translators quite understandably usually charge a minimum amount, perhaps $25, to translate a business letter, and it takes at least a day to deliver it and receive the translation back. In a large company, payment is entangled in paperwork that may well double the price. It is much easier to ask the in-house translator to read the letter on the spot. An in-house translator can also be asked to assist with a phone call abroad or with a document that contains proprietary, sensitive or classified information.

In-house translators are generally considered resources to be called on for any question concerning foreign affairs. This ranges from help in addressing an envelope to assistance with an international conference. While they should not be asked to perform simultaneous interpreting unless they are specially trained for the job, in-house translators can provide informal interpreting services. Most importantly, they offer linguistic and cultural insight that can be vital to hosts who want to avoid causing embarrassment through ignorance of foreign customs.

This same linguistic and cultural insight may be called upon by management for information purposes. In-house translators can scan foreign journals and newspapers and quickly pick out items of interest to company executives, scientists and engineers. Since this is a time-consuming task, the bulk of it will probably be assigned to a computerized SDI (selective dissemination of information) service. However, there are interest profiles that are difficult to fit into a computer program, and in those cases, a well-informed translator can fill in the gaps by scanning selected publications.

Patrons, then, can see the in-house translator as a source of formal translations, informal translations, informal interpretation, and linguistic and cultural insight. However, a company would be foolish to overlook the assistance the in-house translator can offer the library staff.

AIDS TO LIBRARY STAFFS

The most obvious and most common problem the library staff encounters with foreign languages is verification of citations. When a journal title is given with an unusual abbreviation, or two papers by the same author have similar citations, or a citation is given in a non-Roman alphabet, a linguistic specialist can be very helpful. If the library has enough Russian business to justify a subscription to journals such as the *Doklady* of the USSR Academy of Sciences, the people hired as in-house translators will have to be able to read Russian. If the library has many requests for Japanese documents, the translator may be expected to read Japanese as well.

Keep in mind that as little as 15 years ago, Russian was considered an uncommon language, and it was difficult to find anyone at all to translate it. As recently as 1979 the fourth edition of the Professional Services Directory of the American Translators Association (ATA) listed only 89 people who translate from Russian into English, but even that small number appears large when compared to the nine who were listed for Japanese to English translations. (By comparison, there were 245 for German, 285 for French, and 223 for Spanish.) Japanese is as uncommon now as Russian was 15 years ago, but the picture is changing rapidly.

Suppose the librarian has a paper written in a foreign language, and the title must be translated. Is a linguistic specialist needed for such a simple thing as looking up a four-word title in the dictionary? Perhaps it isn't as simple as it looks.

The first question is—which dictionary? Is the language Norwegian, Swedish, Danish, German or Dutch? Spanish, Italian, Portuguese, French or Romanian? Language identification can be tricky, and although there are a number of publications that offer advice, in-house translators can usually offer quicker, surer assistance.[4]

Once the language is identified, the nonexpert may still have an intractable problem. In the Russian alphabet, for example, Z comes before I and G comes before D. Furthermore, the words in the dictionary usually do not exactly match the words being sought, and it is not necessarily obvious which part of the word can be ignored and how the extraneous parts change the meaning of the dictionary entry.

A very basic problem is transliteration of languages that use a non-Roman alphabet. Some transliteration schemes turn a Russian E into English E while others turn it into Ye, for example. There are several of these traps in Cyrillic transliterations, and they can make an on-line search for an author very difficult. A resident linguistic specialist can offer useful advice when the librarian gets that uneasy feeling that something is wrong.

Besides being experts in citations, in-house translators are guides to dictionary selection. It may be that the $29.95 paperback published in East Germany is a masterpiece of lexicography, while the highly-touted $198.50 multilingual tome published in Holland is merely a reprinting of obsolescent terminology from earlier editions. In-house translators, being the ones who will make most use of the dictionary collection, will be valuable assistants in determining where to spend a limited book budget.

So in-house translators can help decipher references, translate foreign titles, identify languages, and select dictionaries. What else can they do for the library staff?

One of the most important problems a library faces in handling requests for translations is selection of a contract translator. Having in-house translators doesn't completely remove that problem, as we have said, because there are always languages or jobs that can't be handled adequately in-house. Since the company wants the best translation it can get for the money it has to spend, someone has to evaluate the work of the available contract translators. Accuracy is perhaps the most important criterion of translation quality, and it is very difficult for a monolingual reader to judge. In-house translators can not only evaluate quality, they can serve as liaison between contract translator and company by providing the translator with specialized reference material and answering questions to help produce a better job.

In summary, in-house translators are quickly available, offer flexible services, and have much better knowledge of company operations, product or research areas than a contract translator. They provide important support to the library staff as well as the patrons. Work assigned to them will be of consistent quality.

DISADVANTAGES

It would not be fair to stop here without pointing out the disadvantages of in-house translators. In particular, if the total volume of translation work is relatively small, in-house translators become an expensive luxury unless they can be usefully employed in another capacity part-time. If they can be employed full-time, however, their cost should be at least competitive with outside translation services.[5] That cost will be difficult to measure, however, because it includes fringe benefits and support costs as well as direct salary. Since in-house translators are asked to provide so many varied services, it will not be easy to figure their productivity either.

Finally, there is one more aspect to the question of availability. If a company has only one in-house translator, as many do, there will be times when that person is unavailable, either because of sickness, vacation, or another job assignment. A science and technology library trying to provide translation services year-round would do well to have a judicious mix of bureau and free-lance on call.

This article has attempted to point out some of the ways in which in-house translators can fit into the information services provided by a science and technology library in an age of increasing specialization. Not every library has enough translation requests to justify an in-house translator, but when the volume begins to approach that level, it is useful to be aware of some of the less obvious ways in which linguistic expertise can be employed.

LITERATURE CITED

1. Draper, R.L., Role of commercial translation firms in providing technical material to sci-tech libraries. *Science & Technology Libraries.* 3(2):21-30; 1982 Winter.

2. Tillinghast, Grace. Survey of in-house translators. *ATA Chronicle.* 12(1-2):13; 1983.

3. Teague, Ben; Teague, Fran. Technical writing and translation. *Journal of Technical Writing and Communication.* 12(2):93-102; 1982.

4. a) Piette, J. R. F.; Horzelska, E. *A guide to foreign languages for science librarians and bibliographers.* London: Aslib; 1965.

   b) Ingle, N. C. A language identification table. *The Incorporated Linguist.* 14(4):98-101; 1976 Autumn.

   c) Newman, P. E. The librarian's field guide to foreign languages. Albuquerque, NM: Sandia National Laboratories; SAND 83- (in press).

5. Gingold, Kurt. The in-house translator in U.S. industry. *Technical Communication.* 29(4):8-10, 1982 Fourth Quarter.

SCI-TECH ONLINE

Ellen Nagle, Editor

DATABASE NEWS

Computer-Readable Numeric Databases Available

The National Bureau of Standards' Office of Standard Reference Data is expanding its program for numeric database dissemination by making available four databases in magnetic tape form. The tapes, which can be mounted on an interactive system, are the *NIH/ EPA/MSDC Mass Spectral Database, Thermophysical Properties of Hydrocarbon Mixtures Database, NBS Chemical Thermodynamic Database,* and the *NBS Crystal Identification File.* The databases have a wide variety of uses, permitting identification of chemical unknowns encountered in different environments, prediction of chemical reaction equilibria, and analysis of heat transfer processes.

The *NIH/EPA/MSDC Mass Spectral Database* contains electron ionization mass spectra of almost 40,000 different compounds. Each spectrum is described by compound name, molecular formula, molecular weight, and Chemical Abstracts Service (CAS) Registry number. A "Quality Index" value is assigned to each spectrum.

The mass spectral data have been collected from a variety of sources through the cooperation of the NBS, the National Institutes of Health, the Environmental Protection Agency and the U.K. Mass Spectrometry Data Centre. Updates will be made available.

The *Thermophysical Properties of Hydrocarbon Mixtures Database (TRAPP)* predicts density, viscosity, and thermal conductivity of hydrocarbon mixtures of arbitrary composition using a tested model and its associated computer software.

The *NBS Chemical Thermodynamic Database* contains recommended values of selected thermodynamic properties for over 15,000 inorganic substances and C_1 and C_2 hydrocarbons. Each data entry gives the chemical name and formula as well as the physical state.

The *NBS Crystal Data Identification File* contains data characterizing over 60,000 crystalline substances. Data include reduced cell parameters, reduced cell volume, space group number and symbol, experimental and calculated density, chemical type classification, and chemical name and formula. The database will be updated.

For further information, contact: National Bureau of Standards, Attn: C. Goldman, Phys. Bldg, Room A320, Washington, DC 20234, Telephone: (301) 921-2228.

Mental Measurements Yearbook Online

The eighth edition of the *Mental Measurements Yearbook,* a standard reference source to assist in the selection of tests for education, psychology, and industry is now online in full-text format at BRS. Produced by the Buros Institute of Mental Measurements, the *Yearbook* provides factual information, critical reviews, population, test level, validity-reliability information and full-text retrieval for all 1184 English language tests covered. Frequent updates, including tests destined for the ninth edition are planned. The database will have a royalty charge of $30 per connect hour. Offline printing charges are $.75 per citation.

CANCEREXPRESS: A New Current Awareness Database

CANCEREXPRESS was made available to the National Library of Medicine (NLM) online network in June 1983. Also known as *EXPRESS,* this file contains bibliographic records identifying articles covering all aspects of the therapy, etiology, and biology of cancer as well as studies of mutagenic agents and agents that stimulate cell division. Records are derived from monthly SDLINE updates using a search profile developed by the National Cancer Institute (NCI) and the National Library of Medicine (NLM). *EXPRESS* is one of a series of technical information products prepared for cancer researchers by the International Cancer Research Data Bank (ICRDB) Program of the NCI in cooperation with the NLM.

EXPRESS is a companion file to *CANCERLIT,* which is a comprehensive archival file of 350,000 bibliographic records to cancer-related documents published since 1963 in several thousand biomedical journals and other publications. In contrast, *EXPRESS* is a more selective, current file containing some 10,000 records from cancer-related articles in several hundred high quality journals published during the most recent four-month period. Records entered into *EXPRESS* are simultaneously entered into the *CANCERLIT* file so they will be included in more comprehensive searches. Records are dropped from *EXPRESS* after four months but are retained in *CANCERLIT.*

Records are entered into *EXPRESS* in the shortest possible time, with a target date of within one month after journal receipt at NLM. All records selected for *EXPRESS* have author abstracts and most have an author address, or at least an organizational affiliation. The citations originate from a group of 180 core journals identified by the NCI as being of high quality and having a high yield of relevant articles. It is anticipated that *EXPRESS* will also be mounted and searched in cancer centers, and test tapes have been requested for this purpose. Availability of *EXPRESS* through commercial vendors is also contemplated.

Mental Health Abstracts Available Online

Mental Health Abstracts is now being offered by DIALOG, as File 86. This database was originally prepared by the National Clearinghouse for Mental Health Information of the U.S. National Institute of Mental health (NIMH) during the years 1969 to 1982. After the NIMH ceased to update the file, the IFL/Plenum Data Company took over the preparation of indexes and abstracts for the updates beginning in 1983. IFL/Plenum will continue to produce and maintain this file. The IFL/Plenum 1983+ updates will only be available online. There is no printed counterpart to this database.

Mental Health Abstracts includes abstracted information on all aspects of mental health and mental illness. Major subject areas covered include psychology, psychiatry, social issues, epidemiology, sexology, psychopharmacology, child development, crime and delinquency, aging, and mental health. It is international in scope and contains articles, books, research reports, manpower studies, dissertations, conference proceedings, and program data in fields relevant to mental health. Over 1,000 periodicals including law school reviews and journals are indexed and abstracted for inclusion in this database.

The file contains approximately 475,000 records from 1969 to the present; about 85% of the articles are in English. The cost for searching the file is $55 per connect hour, $.15 per full record printed offline, and $.05 for each full record printed online.

New Database on Chemical Exposure

Chemical Exposure, a comprehensive database of chemicals that have been identified in human tissues and body fluids, and in feral and food animals, is available from DIALOG. The database is prepared by the Chemical Effects information Center at Oak Ridge National Laboratory by funding agreements among the U.S. Environmental Protection Agency, National Cancer Institute and Department of Energy. The file is meant to provide a centralized resource of body-burden information. Body burden is a reflection of exposures to food, air, and water contaminants as well as pharmaceuticals. The systematic acquisition of body-burden data gives an assessment of human exposure to toxic chemicals and xenobiotics. *Chemical Exposure* corresponds to two print publications: *Chemicals Identified in Human Biological Media* (1978+) and *Chemicals Identified in Feral and Food Animals* (1981+).

Chemical Exposure is bibliographic in nature, containing references to selected articles from over 1,000 journals, conferences, and reports. Items represented in the file include information on approximately 575 chemicals. In each record, the data in the articles has been analyzed and arranged according to type of information, e.g., chemical data: chemical properties, synonyms, CAS registry numbers, formulas; tissue measured: range and mean concentration. The database can be used to find studies on the health effects of particular chemicals, to examine reports of contaminants in a particular region, and to find information on the toxicity of particular pesticides or pharmaceuticals.

Available as File 138, *Chemical Exposure* contains approximately 4000 records from 1974 to the present. It will be updated annually with 2000 records. The price for searching the file is $45 per connect hour and $.15 full record printed offline.

SEARCH SYSTEM NEWS

Lockheed Corporate Reorganization Announced

DIALOG, a wholly owned subsidiary of the Lockheed Corporation, was one of 24 companies and corporate staff organizations that reported directly to the corporate headquarters. In April 1983, the Lockheed Corporation announced a major reorganization of the corporation. The new organization has created four groups of Lockheed companies, each headed by a group president. The four groups are: Aeronautical Systems; Missiles, Space, and Electronics Systems; Marine Systems; and Information Systems. DIALOG Information Services is the largest company in the new Information Systems Group, which reports directly to corporate headquarters. According to DIALOG, "The formation of this group as one of the major components in Lockheed corporate organization represents a strong and continuing commitment by Lockheed to information systems. We are very pleased with this change of direction."

SDC Search Service Becomes SDC Information Services

SDC recently announced an expanded business direction under a new name, SDC Information Services. It plans to address knowledge specialists' needs with a broadened offering of products and services for research information management. According to SDC, the name change signals "SDC's move toward making available computer-based capabilities in the form of research support systems." Product offerings include online computer processing, software program products and professional system support.

PUBLICATIONS AND SEARCH AIDS

Descriptive Materials for Chemical and Toxicological Files Available

NLM's Specialized Information Services (SIS) Division has several new explanatory materials available about the NLM Chemical and Toxicological files. These are:

A "SAMPLER," which is a 25-page booklet that describes

the databases to new or prospective users and provides annotated search examples. Copies are available at no cost from SIS.

A Slide/Tape Overview that describes the files and support services provided by SIS, and gives sample searches for each file. The presentation contains thirty-nine 35mm slides with a 15-minute audiocassette. An abbreviated version, which does not have the sample searches, is also available. It contains 16 slides with a 5-minute cassette.

An 11" × 14" multi-colored poster that gives a diagrammatic overview of the files and would be an appropriate handout at meetings, demonstrations, and training sessions. Copies of the poster are available without cost from SIS.

Updated versions of the pocket cards for each of the NLM Chemical and Toxicological files are available at no charge from SIS.

For further information, or to order any of these items, contact: Specialized Information Services, National Library of Medicine, Bldg. 38A, Rm. 3S320, Bethesda, MD 20209, (301) 496-1131.

SCI-TECH IN REVIEW

Suzanne Fedunok, Editor

NEW TOOL IN SCIENCE, TECHNOLOGY AND SOCIETY

White, Howard D., Griffith, Belver C. Authors as markers of intellectual space: co-citation in studies of science, technology and society. *Journal of Documentation.* 38(4): 255-272; 1982 December.

The authors, with the School of Library and Information Science at Drexel University, offer "a new tool," that of co-citation analysis, to authors and specialists in the field of science, technology and society. Their study of how seventy-one authors in this field are related resulted in the creation of "a space of intellectual activity" derived from objective data (co-citation frequencies based on the frequency with which new papers co-cite the work of two authors) manipulated by multivariate statistical analysis and displayed in a computer-generated visual format. The authors compared their results with a view of the relationships and importance of specialists in the field described by I. Spiegel-Rosing and D. DeS. Price in their book *Science, technology and society* [London: Sage, 1977], and feel that this method results in a more clear and definite picture of the topic.

Perhaps the most interesting part of the study was the figures, computer-generated visual displays showing relatedness in terms of "peaks, ridges, and troughs," which are used to describe the connections between various subjects in the field of science, technology and society and between influential specialists.

THE TRUTH OF SCIENTIFIC INQUIRY

Pollet, Miriam. Criteria for science book selection in academic libraries. *Collection Building.* 4(3): 42-47; 1982.

The author is science bibliographer in the library of Brooklyn College, CUNY. She maintains that "the first criterion in judging science books is the integrity of the intellectual content," with the understanding that truth in science is never certain. The rapidly changing nature of science makes selection difficult, as does the tendency of respected scientists to pretend to expertise in areas beyond their scientific competence. For these reasons, among others mentioned, the author points out that while selectors in the sciences may seem to be acting as censors, which goes against the liberal ideal of libraries, in fact "in the sciences we are in a different realm of 'truth'; it cannot be determined by individual immediate experience . . . we must apply different criteria to science books— or reject the notion of science entirely." She concludes that the most important factor in science book selection is in fact the informed and expert selector.

LIBRARY COMMITTEES

Katayama, Jane H. Library committee; how important is it? *Special Libraries.* 74(1): 44-48; 1983 January.

The author describes her positive experience with library committees at M.I.T.'s Lincoln Laboratory. She suggests beginning with a formal written charter to make clear the committee's purpose, membership, and functions, which she lists as advising, supporting and guiding the library director, and serving as liaison between the library and management. In the author's view, library committees provide important benefits such as technical expertise, moral support, and advice on major projects and decisions; they can also act as advocates among their colleagues for innovations and changes.

TEACHING SCIENCE LIBRARIANSHIP

Wilson, Concepcion S. Teaching science bibliography: from classroom to marketplace. *Journal of Education for Librarianship.* 23(2): 125-136; 1982 Fall.

The author, who is a lecturer at the University of New South Wales School of Librarianship, describes a pilot program there which is designed to give students a realistic experience of being a science librarian. Students were assigned the task of interviewing researchers to determine their information needs and of compiling relevant bibliographies for them. The experience of the students was evaluated by questionnaires seeking information on their satisfaction with the program, and by evaluating the bibliographies produced. The students' work was compared with that of the previous class, in terms of user satisfaction, relevance, recall and amount of new material found.

The author concludes with several suggestions for improvement of the program, and comments on its success: "The academic community offers a convenient and willing laboratory for librarianship students interested in testing their information-handling skills. One wonders whether an even wider range of communities—e.g., business, government, industrial, commercial—may not be amenable to inclusion in such programs if they were approached by library schools." The program also offered those students with strong subject background in the sciences some attractive alternatives to traditional library work—that of being specialist on a research team, for example—as well as to promote and publicize library services among scientists (one-third of whom reported that they were unaware of the indexing and abstracting services available at the University of New South Wales).

CHEMISTS AND INFORMATION SERVICES

Chemical firms rank high in information services. *Chemical and Engineering News*. 61(16): 18-20; 1983 April 18.

This is a summary of a report made by Eugene B. Jackson, a professor at the University of Texas at Austin's Graduate School of Library and Information Sciences, to the Division of Chemical Information section of the American Chemical Society at their Symposium on the Cost of Providing Information from an Industrial Information Center.

The report showed that the chemical industry spends about 2% of its R & D budget on technical information services, which is the highest percentage the author discovered in his study, and that the industry leads in the number of libraries, number of companies with international library systems, number of professional librarians, ratio of libraries to employees, and "library penetration" (a measure of company spending on information services).

The information in the study was extrapolated from data sources such as standard directories, professional society surveys, indexes of literature and materials costs, and reports of corporate R & D spending. Chemical industry budgets for information services are generally considered proprietary and confidential. The article includes a table showing dollar figures for the top four firms, "other firms," and total expenditures for such categories as books, periodicals, document delivery, online services, personnel and facilities.

SCIENTISTS VIEW INFORMATION

Rowland, J.F.B. Scientist's view of his information system. *Journal of Documentation.* 38(1): 38-42; 1982 March.

In this paper the author reports on that part of the Royal Society of London study that dealt with a survey of the views of the scientific community on scientific information. A series of samples of respondents were selected from among biological scientists, physical scientists, physicists, and biologists, biochemists and chemists in four different kinds of research settings. A lengthy questionnaire was administered to them, and the results summarized in this paper.

The author comes to the conclusion that the scientists questioned were a rather conservative group. "Most of these scientists search for information for both current and retrospective awareness by searching directly in the journals themselves. Faced with five possible innovations in the publication of scientific papers, they gave positive approval to only the least radical, printing from camera-ready copy."

In contrast to this conservatism, however, the author discovered that most scientists were happy with the quality and quantity of reviews in their fields, they did not object to the proliferation of scientific journals or to the increased specialization of journals; they did not support publication of papers as separates. They were interested in computer-based information retrieval, but fewer than half of them had used it, largely due to lack of access to terminals and of suitable training. About a quarter of the scientists surveyed found the electronic journal an acceptable alternative, "a surprisingly high proportion of respondents."

SCIENTIFIC INFORMATION IN THE U.K.

Rowland, J.F.B. Economic position of some British primary scientific journals. *Journal of Documentation.* 38(2): 94-106; 1982 June.

This is the final paper in a series of reports in this journal on the study conducted by the Royal Society of London on the scientific information system in the United Kingdom between 1978 and 1981. This section details the examination of the financial state of a range of primary scientific journals published by British learned societies from 1972 to 1980. It includes tabular information gathered by the study on prices, circulation, number of papers submitted, number of pages published, and fiscal accounts, but as the information solicited was provided under a guarantee of confidentiality, the study refers only to "Societies 1,2,3 and 4." The author's summary of the study includes the following statements: "Taking an average view of the different publications, one can see that a typical publication was increasing its price rapidly, increasing its number of pages somewhat, and increasing its price per page slightly faster than general inflation . . . circulation was falling. Yet healthy surpluses were accruing. The number of papers submitted continued to rise and the proportion of them accepted is perhaps falling very slightly. And, during uncertain economic conditions, the surpluses of the major societies on their publishing programs have increased enormously."

For Product Safety Concerns and Information please contact our EU representative GPSR@taylorandfrancis.com
Taylor & Francis Verlag GmbH, Kaufingerstraße 24, 80331 München, Germany